The Freshwater Angler™

Luring Largemouth
BASS

By Don Oster

Surefire Strategies
for Catching
More and Bigger Bass

CREATIVE
PUBLISHING
international

MINNETONKA, MINNESOTA

CREDITS

Creative Publishing international, Inc.
5900 Green Oak Drive
Minnetonka, MN 55343
1-800-328-3895

President/CEO: David D. Murphy
Vice President/Editorial: Patricia K. Jacobsen
Vice President/Retail Sales & Marketing: Richard M. Miller

LURING LARGEMOUTH BASS
By Don Oster

Executive Editor, Outdoor Group: Don Oster
Editorial Director: David R. Maas
Senior Editor: David L. Tieszen
Technical Advisor: John Hudgens
Managing Editor: Jill Anderson
Creative Director: Brad Springer
Senior Art Director: David W. Schelitzche
Mac Designer: Joe Fahey
Photo Researcher: Angela Hartwell
Director, Production Services: Kim Gerber
Production Staff: Laura Hokkanen, Kay Swanson

Illustrator: Dennis Rogers

Contributor: Ranger boats

Printed on American paper by: R. R. Donnelley & Sons Co.

10 9 8 7 6 5 4 3 2 1

ISBN 0-86573-117-9

CONTENTS

INTRODUCTION

More American anglers pursue large-mouth bass than any other freshwater gamefish. The main reason: bass fishing is exciting. Once you experience the head-shaking leap of a largemouth, chances are you will come back for more.

One measure of the largemouth's appeal is the huge number of anglers that belong to bass-fishing organizations such as the Bass Anglers Sportsman Society (B.A.S.S.).

Most of these fishermen can find bass within a short drive from home. Largemouths are found in waters from southern Canada to the tropics. They live in muddy rivers and crystal-clear lakes, tiny golf course ponds and 100-mile-long reservoirs, knee-deep sloughs and even brackish coastal estuaries alongside saltwater fish.

The purpose of this book is to make you a better bass fisherman. It leads you through the world of bass fishing with a clear, concise text and spectacular photographs, many of which provide rare underwater glimpses of bass in their favorite hiding spots. You'll see where to find bass, how they strike and what you must do to hook them.

The first requirement for catching bass is understanding the fish. This book explains every important aspect of largemouth behavior based on input from prominent bass scientists. You will discover how bass detect food, what they eat and when they are likely to feed. After studying the results of a unique laboratory experiment, you will understand why finding cover is vital to catching bass.

In most waters, only a small fraction of the acreage contains bass. To catch largemouths consistently, you must know where to look at different times of the day and year, and under different weather conditions.

The equipment section will help you select everything from boats and motors to rods and reels. Not everyone needs a high-powered bass boat; sometimes a small, portable boat or float tube works better. But a serious bass fisherman should own a depth finder and know how to use it in conjunction with a lake map. This section will also show you how to choose the right lure or bait, and how to find the best retrieve.

Most bass fishermen know how to catch largemouths in their favorite lake when conditions are right. But if the weather changes or if they try a different lake, they fail to make the necessary adjustments. The section titled "Special Situations" will show you how to find bass quickly and how to make them bite in almost every conceivable situation. Included are dozens of proven techniques, plus many little-known secrets used by the country's bass experts.

The final section, "Putting It All Together," from the editors of The Freshwater Angler, explains how to catch bass throughout the year in five of the country's top-notch bass fisheries. You may never spend time on one of these bodies of water, but you can apply the specific tips and techniques to catch bass on similar fisheries in your area.

Whether you do most of your fishing in tiny farm ponds or sprawling reservoirs, whether you're a beginner or a veteran, this book is sure to improve your bass-fishing skills.

1

●●●●●●●●●●●●●●●●●●

THE LARGEMOUTH
BASS

All About Bass

Renowned for its explosive strikes and spectacular leaps, the largemouth bass is a favorite among millions of freshwater fishermen.

Largemouths were originally found only east of the Mississippi River and south of the Great Lakes. But as bass fishing grew in popularity, so did stocking programs in many states. Largemouths are now caught in waters throughout the continental United States and Hawaii, in addition to southern Canada and most of Mexico. Bass have been introduced in Europe, Asia, Africa and South America.

The largemouth bass is the largest member of a group of closely related fishes called *black bass*. Others include the smallmouth, spotted, redeye, Suwannee and Guadalupe. The largemouth is distinguished from all of these species by a jaw that extends beyond the eye. All black bass belong to the sunfish family, but differ from sunfish because of their longer bodies.

Biologists have identified two subspecies of largemouth bass: the Florida largemouth and the northern largemouth. Originally, Florida bass lived only in Florida waters. Stocking efforts have expanded their range to include much of the South, particularly Texas and California.

Although they look alike, the Florida largemouth grows considerably larger than the northern subspecies. A trophy Florida bass weighs from 10 to 12 pounds, compared to 6 to 8 pounds for a northern largemouth bass.

Some biologists believe that the world-record largemouth bass was a cross between the northern and Florida subspecies. The 22-pound, 4-ounce largemouth was caught in June, 1932, at Montgomery Lake in Georgia. This lake is one of many waters in Georgia and Alabama where largemouth crosses have been found.

Largemouths vary in color, depending upon the type of water. Bass from murky waters are pale, while those from clear waters are darker. Largemouths range from deep green to pale olive across the back, with bellies that are a

Lateral Line

shade of white or yellow. All bass have a black lateral band that runs from the head to tail. The band becomes more distinct when a fish is exposed to sunlight, but may disappear when a largemouth is in deep or murky water.

SENSES. Largemouth bass have the five major senses common to most animals: hearing, sight, smell, taste and touch. They have another sense, the *lateral line*, which is a series of sensitive nerve endings that extends from just behind the gill to the tail on each side of the fish.

The lateral line can pick up underwater vibrations as subtle as a swimming baitfish. In one experiment, researchers placed small cups over the eyes of bass, then dropped minnows into a tank with the largemouths. Eventually the bass ate each minnow, using their lateral lines to locate the baitfish. This experiment suggests that bass can detect a lure in the murkiest water.

Largemouth bass hear with internal ears located within the skull. They may be attracted by the ticking or popping of some artificial lures. But when they hear loud, unfamiliar sounds, they usually swim to deeper water or cover. Many bass fishermen carpet the bottoms of their boats to reduce noise that might spook the fish.

Bass can see in all directions, except directly below or behind. In clear water, they can see 30 feet or more. But in most bass waters, visibility is limited to 5 to 10 feet. Largemouths can also see objects that are above water. To avoid spooking fish, many fishermen wear neutral-colored clothing that blends with the background.

Bass in shallow water can detect colors, especially red. In one study, red and white lures caught three times as many largemouths as any other color. Color selection is less important in deep water because most colors appear as shades of gray.

Most experts are reluctant to say that one color is always better than another. The best colors vary, depending on light conditions, water clarity and water color. Most believe that a lure's action is more important than its color.

The eye of a largemouth absorbs more light than does the human eye, enabling the fish to see its food in dim light or darkness. Bass will feed at any time of the day or night, but are less inclined to leave cover and search for food under bright conditions. Like most fish, they prefer shade. They find better ambush camouflage in shady spots or under low-light conditions.

Largemouths smell through nostrils, or *nares*, on the snout. The nares are short passageways through which water is drawn and expelled without entering the throat. Like most fish, bass can detect minute amounts of scent in the water. However, bass rely on scent less than catfish, salmon or trout.

Bass use their sense of touch to determine whether to reject or swallow an object. They will usually hold on to a soft-bodied, artificial worm longer than a metal lure.

Sense of taste is not as important to largemouth bass as it is to some fish species, because bass have few taste cells in their mouths.

FEEDING. Newly hatched largemouths feed heavily on tiny crustaceans and other zooplankton until the bass reach 2 inches in length. Young largemouths eat insects and small fish, including smaller bass. Adult largemouths

prey mostly on fish, but crayfish, frogs and insects are important foods in some waters.

Wherever they live, bass rank high in the aquatic food chain. A bass 10 inches or longer has few enemies and will eat almost anything it can swallow. Because of its large mouth and flexible stomach, a bass can eat prey nearly half its own length.

Largemouths *inhale* small foods. The bass opens its mouth quickly to suck in water and the food. It then forces the water out the gills while it either swallows or rejects the object. Bass can expel food as quickly as they inhale it, so anglers must set the hook immediately when using small lures or baits.

Bass usually grab large prey, then turn the food to swallow it headfirst. This explains why anglers who use large golden shiners, frogs or salamanders wait a minute or two before setting the hook.

As the water warms, the metabolism of bass increases and they feed more often. Largemouths seldom eat at water temperatures below 50°F. From 50° to 68°F, feeding increases and from 68° to 80°F, they feed heavily. However, at temperatures above 80°F, feeding declines.

No one is certain what causes bass to strike artificial lures or bait. Experts point to hunger as the main reason. However, many of these same experts believe that reflex, aggressiveness, curiosity and competitiveness may play a part.

Reflex, or a sudden instinctive reaction, may explain why a bass with a full stomach strikes an artificial lure the instant it hits the water. The fish has little time to judge what it is grabbing, yet some cue triggers it to strike.

Male bass display aggressiveness when they attack lures or chase other fish that invade their nest sites. Although this behavior is common during nesting season, bass are not as aggressive at other times of the year.

Curiosity may be the reason that bass rush up to inspect new objects or sounds. However, it is doubtful they take food solely out of curiosity. Competitiveness probably explains why fishermen occasionally catch two bass on the same lure at the same time. Often several bass race to devour a single food item, particularly in waters where food is in short supply.

GROWTH. The best trophy bass waters are those where the fish grow rapidly as a result of proper temperatures and abundant food. Largemouths seldom reach large sizes in waters where they have become too abundant.

The amount bass grow in a year depends on the length of their *growing season,* or the number of days suitable for growth. The growing season in the South may last twice as long as it does in the North. For example, in 4 years, the average Louisiana largemouth reaches about 18 inches, an Illinois bass is about 13 inches, while a Wisconsin bass averages about 11 inches. Largemouths gain weight most quickly in water from 75° to 80°F. They do not grow in water colder than 50°F.

Although bass in the South grow and mature faster, they rarely live as long as largemouths in colder, northern lakes. In southern waters, bass occasionally reach 10 years of age; in northern waters, bass may live as long as 15 years.

TINY BASS FRY are usually protected by the male bass.

Female bass live longer than males, so they are more apt to reach a trophy size. In one study, 30 percent of the females were 5 years or older, while only 9 percent of the male bass were 5 years or more.

Spawning Behavior

In spring, when inshore waters reach about 60°F, large-mouth bass swim onto spawning grounds in shallow bays, backwaters, channels and other areas protected from prevailing winds. Spawning grounds usually have firm bottoms of sand, gravel, mud or rock. The sticky eggs adhere to bottom and the roots of plants. Bass seldom nest on a thick layer of silt. Some spawning areas are in open water; others have sparse weeds, boulders or logs.

Male bass may spend several days selecting their nest sites. The beds are usually in 1 to 4 feet of water, but may be deeper in clear water. Most largemouths nest in pockets in bulrushes, water lilies or other weeds. Bass in open areas often select a site on the sunny side of a submerged log or large rock. The males seldom nest where they can see another

nesting male. For this reason, beds are generally at least 30 feet apart, but may be closer if weeds, boulders, sunken logs or stumps prevent the males from seeing each other.

Largemouths spawn when the water reaches 63° to 68°F and temperatures remain within this range for several days. Cold fronts may cause water temperatures to drop, which interrupts and delays spawning.

Preparing the nest, the male largemouth shakes its head and tail to sweep away bottom debris. The typical nest is a saucer-shaped depression about 2 to 3 feet in diameter, or twice the length of the male.

Spawning occurs as the male and female move over the nest with their vents close together. The male bumps and nips the female, stimulating her to deposit the eggs. Then the male covers the eggs with his sperm, or *milt*.

A female bass lays from 2,000 to 7,000 eggs per pound of body weight. She may deposit all of her eggs in one nest or drop them at several different sites before leaving the spawning grounds. After spawning, the female recuperates in deep water, where she does not eat for 2 to 3 weeks.

Alone on the nest, the male hovers above the eggs, slowly fanning them to keep off silt and debris and to circulate oxygen-rich water over the eggs. He does not eat while guarding the eggs, but will attack other fish that swim near the nest. The male will not attack slow-moving objects, such as a crayfish or even a plastic worm. Instead, he gently picks up the object and drops it outside the nest.

Sunfish often prey on bass eggs or newly hatched *fry*. In waters with large sunfish populations, the panfish can seriously hamper bass reproduction. A school of sunfish surrounds a nest, and while the male chases some away, others invade the nest and devour the eggs or fry. Cover such as weeds, stumps, logs and rocks provides extra protection for the eggs and fry. Bass that build their nests next to these objects have less area to guard against sunfish and other predators.

Bass eggs hatch in only 2 days at 72°F, but take 5 days at 67°F. Cold weather following spawning will delay hatching. If the shallows drop to 50°F, the fry will not emerge for 13 days. At lower temperatures, the eggs fail to develop. A

HOW BASS RELATE TO FEATURES IN A CONTROLLED LOCATION EXPERIMENT

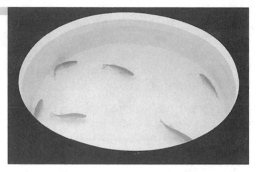

A PLAIN WHITE TANK lacks features. Lighting is evenly distributed and sounds carefully controlled. These 2-pound bass swim about aimlessly.

A BOARD over one edge of the tank provides acceptable cover for the bass. The fish station themselves in the shade under the board.

severe cold front sometimes causes males to abandon the nest, resulting in a complete loss of eggs or fry. From 2,000 to 12,000 eggs hatch from the typical nest. Of these, only five to ten are likely to survive to reach 10 inches in length. After hatching, the tiny fry lie in the nest for 8 to 10 days. Once they are able to swim, the fry remain in a compact school, hovering beneath weeds or other overhead cover. As the fry grow larger, they spread over a wider area, but the male still protects them. The male abandons they fry when they reach about 1 inch in length. After that, he may eat any fry he encounters.

Habitat Requirements

Largemouth bass have certain habitat requirements that are important to their survival.

ROCKS piled in one area of the tank attract the bass immediately. They form a closely-packed school above and along the edge of the rock pile.

A BLACK STRIPE painted on the wall provides something to which bass can relate. They hover near the stripe, even though it offers no cover.

TEMPERATURE. Many studies of bass behavior have concluded that largemouths prefer water temperatures of 77° to 86°F. But fishermen know that bass often bite better in water at lower temperatures, even when water in their preferred temperature range is available. This is explained by the fact that bass will abandon an area with ideal temperature to escape bright sunlight or to find food or cover. Bass cannot survive at temperatures above 98°F.

OXYGEN. Bass require more oxygen than most other gamefish. All lakes have sufficient oxygen in the shallows. But in *fertile* lakes, those with a high level of nutrients, the depths may lack oxygen. Fertile lakes produce large amounts of plankton. These tiny plants and animals eventually die and sink to bottom where they decompose. The decomposition process consumes huge amounts of oxygen, making the depths unsuitable for fish. Heavy algae blooms are a symptom of high water fertility.

In the North, fertile lakes may *winter-kill*. Thick ice and snow cover block out sunlight, so plants can no longer produce oxygen. Decomposition continues, drawing all oxygen from even the shallowest water. Bass are one of the first to die in winterkill lakes. In deep, clear waters such as canyon reservoirs and strip pits, water fertility is usually low. The water contains ample oxygen from top to bottom, so bass can move wherever they want.

FEATURES. A feature is any difference in the underwater world, including cover, structure and less obvious differences like current or shadows. Features are more important to bass than to most other gamefish.

Largemouths require cover from the moment they hatch. Bass fry crowd into dense weedbeds to escape predatory fish. Later in their lives, bass use weeds, rocks, flooded timber and brush, sunken logs and other objects for shade, shelter and ambush points. Overhead cover in shallow water provides shade and cooler temperatures, allowing bass to remain all summer. Weedy edges provide points of ambush where bass can dart out to capture smaller fish.

Structure is the geologic makeup of the bottom. It may be a reef, point or any other place where the depth changes. It can also be a rock patch or any other place where the bottom material changes from one type to other. Largemouths use structure as a reference point to guide their daily movements. They also locate near structure simply because it is unique from the rest of the area. In a controlled location experiment, researchers discovered that bass will relate to anything different in their surroundings.

Typical Bass Waters

Largemouths can tolerate a wider range of water clarity, fertility and temperature than any other gamefish. They thrive in waters ranging from desert reservoirs to northern glacial lakes. You're likely to find largemouths in any of the following waters:

RESERVOIRS. Most man-made lakes are created to control downstream flooding or to provide a reliable source of water for municipalities, farming, power generation and river navigation. As a rule, shallow, warm reservoirs with plenty of submerged trees, brush and aquatic plants for cover offer better fishing than deep, cold reservoirs with little cover.

Flatland reservoirs produce more and bigger largemouth bass than other reservoir types. Sometimes called *flowages* in the North, these waters are normally shallow and fertile with low to moderate clarity. Most have short creek arms, abundant weeds and flooded timber and sand or mud bottoms.

Canyon reservoirs, found mainly in the West, are formed by damming large river gorges. Most are very deep and clear with steep walls, sharp-breaking points and long creek arms. Bottoms consist of rock or sand with few plants. Creek arms may have some timber and brush.

Cove reservoirs, also called *hill-land, highland* or *mountain reservoirs*, are intermediate in depth, fertility and clarity, between canyon and flatland types. Creek arms are also intermediate in length. Most have some weeds and timber with sand, rock or clay bottoms.

PONDS AND PITS. Millions of farm ponds have been stocked with largemouth bass, usually in combination with sunfish. Landowners often obtain the fish from state or federal conservation agencies. Bass and sunfish are also planted in pits and quarries, once sand-gravel or mining operations cease and the basins fill with water.

Strip pits usually have sheer walls, jagged bottoms, sharp-breaking points and rock slides. Most have rock or sand bottoms, with clear, infertile water. Strip pits are generally deep with few weeds.

Farm ponds are shallow and fertile. They have mud or clay bottoms and some submerged weeds. Brush piles are added occasionally to provide cover for bass and other gamefish. Runoff keeps most ponds murky.

NATURAL LAKES. Warm, shallow, weedy lakes usually hold more largemouths than deep, cold, clear lakes with little vegetation. However, shallow, weedy bays of deep, cold lakes may hold good largemouth bass populations.

Eutrophic lakes have shallow, fertile water of low to medium clarity. There are extensive stands of submerged and emergent weeds, commonly extending into mid-lake. The bottom is mainly mud, often with patches of sand or gravel. In the North, these lakes may winterkill.

Mesotrophic lakes have moderate depth, fertility and clarity. The shallows are often rimmed with emergent weeds, and submerged weeds may grow to depths of 25 feet. The bottom, which usually consists of sand, gravel, rock and muck, normally has sandy humps or rocky reefs.

RIVERS, STREAMS AND ESTUARIES. Slow-moving rivers and streams with weeds, brush or fallen trees for cover often have excellent largemouth populations. Bass also thrive in the brackish water of *estuaries*, where fresh water from rivers mixes with salt water.

Streams with warm water and deep pools make good bass habitat, particularly when there is an abundance of cover such as weeds and submerged logs, brush or boulders.

Big rivers with weedy backwaters, cuts or bays off the main channel make ideal bass water. Few largemouths are found in the main channel itself because of the swift current.

Estuaries with connecting marshes and canals and an abundance of weeds and water-dwelling trees are well suited to largemouths. Fish location is greatly affected by the tides.

2

WHERE TO FIND
BASS

Bass Movements Through the Seasons

A prominent bass expert once estimated that "80 percent of the challenge in bass fishing is finding the fish." Locating bass may be difficult because seasonal movement patterns differ in almost every body of water. Temperature, oxygen level, food supply and even the angle of the sun's rays have an effect on bass location in each season.

SPRING. Springtime movements of bass center around spawning. Weeks before spawning begins, bass start moving from deep water toward shallows that warm quickly. Males move in first. During this *pre-spawn* period, look for bass near their spawning grounds, but in slightly deeper water. On a warm day, bass will move into the spawning area, even though spawning is weeks away. They retreat to deeper water when the weather cools. They may repeat this pattern often during the pre-spawn period.

Bass begin to feed when the water temperature edges above 50°F, but catching them is difficult until the water reaches about 55°F. Then they begin a feeding binge that is unequaled at any other time of the year. Anglers catch bass in the shallows throughout the day. Baitfish are scarce, so bass spend most of their time cruising shallow water in search of food. And because the sun is at a low angle, light penetration does not force them into deeper water.

Spawning begins when the water reaches the mid-60s. After depositing their eggs, the females abandon the nests. They feed very little for the next 2 to 3 weeks while they recover from spawning. Males guarding their beds will strike lures that come too close.

Water temperatures in the low 70s signal the beginning of the *post-spawn* period and the resumption of good fishing. Females have recovered and males have completed their nest-guarding duties. Both feed heavily in the shallows but spend most of the day in deeper water.

Springtime movements of bass extend from February to April in southern waters. But in the North, they are compressed into just a few weeks, usually from May to early June.

SUMMER. As summer progresses, strong sunlight or warm surface temperatures may force bass out of shallow water. Bass form loose schools along deep structure and cover during midday, but feed in the shallows in morning and evening. Food is easy to find, so feeding periods tend to be short. Some largemouths stay in the shallows all day if the cover is dense enough or the water murky enough to block out sunlight.

Water temperature above 80°F will usually push bass deeper, regardless of water clarity. But in fertile lakes, low oxygen levels in the depths prevent bass from going deeper. They must remain in warm, shallow water, where they become listless and difficult to catch.

FALL AND WINTER. When the water begins to cool in fall, bass in deep water return to the shallows. Early fall is much like the pre-spawn period. In most waters, the summer's predation has reduced their food supply, so bass roam the shallows looking for a meal. And with the sun once again lower in the sky, they can stay shallow all day. But many anglers have quit fishing for the season by the time bass begin their fall feeding binge.

As the surface water continues to cool, it eventually reaches the same temperature as water in the depths. This starts the *fall turnover*. With water at the same temperature and density throughout, wind circulates the lake from top to bottom. Bass may be almost anywhere, so finding them is difficult. In most waters, fall turnover lasts from 1 to 2 weeks.

In late fall, the surface water becomes colder than water in the depths. Bass prefer the warmer water, so they move to deep areas of the lake. They remain in these deepwater haunts through winter, whether or not the lake freezes over.

Temperatures below 50°F make bass sluggish and difficult to catch. But a few days of warm, sunny weather may draw them into the shallows. Fishermen aware of this late season movement can enjoy some of the year's best fishing, especially for big bass. However, if water temperatures fall below 40°F, bass are almost impossible to catch.

Ice fishermen sometimes enjoy a short flurry of action just after freeze-up, but very few largemouths are taken during the rest of winter.

Reservoirs and Natural Lakes: Spring

RESERVOIRS. Creek arms, or *coves*, provide the best spawning habitat in most reservoirs. Bass prefer wide, shallow coves with slightly murky water to those that are deep and clear. Good spawning coves usually have some inflowing water. Adult bass return to traditional spawning areas year after year. If you can find a good cove, chances are that bass will be there the next year.

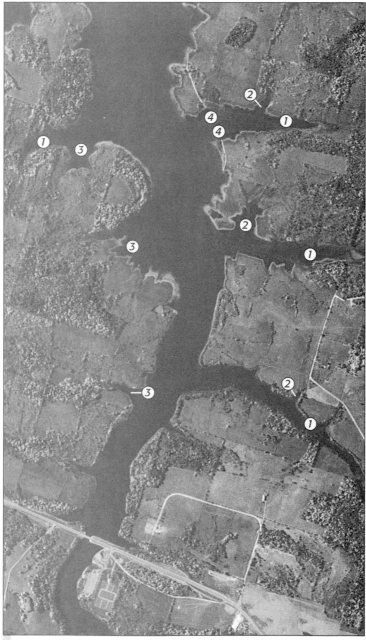

SPAWNING AREAS in reservoirs include: (1) back ends of creek arms, (2) secondary creek arms, (3) small bays along the main channel or in the arms, (4) shallow sections of submerged roads.

Bass wintering in the main river channel of a reservoir may have to swim many miles to find a shallow creek arm suitable for spawning. However, some bass spawn in shallow bays, on mid-lake humps and along brushy shorelines within the main body of the reservoir. These fish do not move as far.

Prior to spawning, bass hang just outside the cove or along the creek channel within the cove. On a warm day, they move into the following areas:

•*Back ends of coves* have the shallowest, warmest water. Bass concentrate along the edge of a creek channel, then spawn in shoreline cover such as brush, timber or weeds.

•*Shoreline breaks* within the main body of the reservoir hold pre-spawn bass. Flooded timber extending far out from shore indicates a wide shoal that warms quickly, attracting many spawners.

•*Sheltered bays* warm faster than open areas. They provide good spawning habitat, especially in canyon reservoirs. The best bays are shallow and contain some cover such as flooded brush.

•*Fingers* projecting off the main cove, such as secondary creek arms or shallow bays, draw spawning bass. Fingers warm earlier than other parts of the cove; check them first for spawning activity.

After spawning, largemouths spend most of their time along the creek channel or near shoreline points before moving back to the main body of the reservoir. How soon they leave a cove after spawning depends on the depth. Some deep coves hold bass through the summer.

NATURAL LAKES. Springtime movements in natural lakes are generally not as dramatic as those in reservoirs. Prior to spawning, bass hold on breaks adjacent to shoreline vegetation or near the mouths of sheltered bays or channels. In a small lake, bass frequently spawn in shallow water bordering their deep wintering sites. But in a large lake, they may have to cross an expanse of open water to find a protected bay or a dead-end channel. In lakes that lack sheltered areas, bass will spawn in shoreline weeds. The following areas are key springtime bass spots:

•*Dead-end channels* are sheltered from wind. The best channels are lined with emergent vegetation and are shallower than 5 feet.

•*Shallow bays* warm faster than the rest of the lake. Mud-bottomed bays warm first because the dark bottom absorbs the sun's rays.

•*Floating vegetation,* such as the roots of lily pads and drifting clumps of cattail or maidencane, provides overhead cover prior to spawning.

•*Lily pads* begin to push toward the surface before bass start to spawn. The pads offer excellent cover for adult largemouths and their newly hatched fry.

•*Bulrushes* and other loosely spaced emergent vegetation attract spawning bass. Bass often build their nests in the middle of bulrush stands.

•*Maidencane,* or other emergent plants that grow in dense stands, provides good spawning cover. Look for nests in open pockets or along the edge of the weeds.

Reservoirs and Natural Lakes: Summer

RESERVOIRS. Bass location can vary widely during summer, depending on the type of reservoir. In clear canyon reservoirs of the Southwest, anglers routinely catch bass in 40 to 50 feet of water. But in murky flatland reservoirs, most bass are taken from water 15 feet or shallower.

Some flatland reservoirs have wide expanses of shallow water that become too warm for bass during the hottest part of summer. Deep creek channels offer the only cool water. Bass sometimes move as deep as 25 feet if the water is relatively clear.

Cove reservoirs offer a variety of bass habitat. Deep coves may hold as many bass as the main river channel. Bass also collect along shoreline points or rocky shelves with flooded brush, and on humps just off the main channel. Look for bass in water less than 30 feet deep. Despite warm surface temperatures, bass in cove and flatland reservoirs usually feed in the shallows early and late in the day.

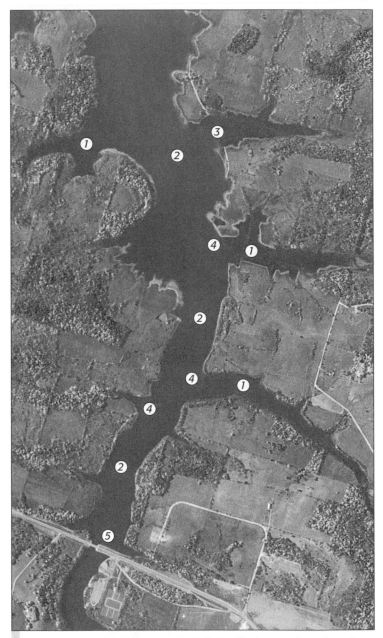

SUMMER LOCATIONS in reservoirs include: (1) deep sections of creek channels, (2) the main river channel, (3) deep areas of submerged roads, (4) points along the main body of the reservoir, (5) riprap on an embankment.

30

Canyon reservoirs have little bass cover. Most lack flooded timber or brush. If you can find some, you are almost sure to catch fish. They also gather along points, in the shade of sheer walls or where the cliff face has caved in, creating an underwater rock slide.

In reservoirs with large populations of shad, schools of small bass spend much of their time following the baitfish. The bass corner the shad against a line of brush or timber, or push them toward the surface. Fishermen occasionally spot bass breaking the surface over open water far from cover or structure.

Regardless of the reservoir type, always check out the following areas for summertime bass:

•*Cliffs* with uneven faces hold more bass than those with smooth, straight walls. Look for crevices, caves, ledges or rock slides. Bass frequently hang near a tree or brush on the cliff face.

•*Points* with large rocks, flooded timber or brush draw more largemouths than those with little cover. In summer, bass feed on points near creek channels, then drop into deep water after feeding.

•*Green leaves* on newly flooded vegetation provide excellent cover for bass. The leaves block out sunlight and attract many types of bass food.

•*Outside bends* of creek channels or the main channel are usually deeper and hold more bass than inside turns or straight sections.

•*Brushy flats* serve as feeding areas. Flats with deep holes and abundant cover are better than large flats with uniform depth and little cover.

Reservoirs, and also deep lakes, form distinct temperature layers in summer. The bottom layer is coolest, but often lacks oxygen. The middle layer, or *thermocline*, is a zone where the temperature changes rapidly. Bass are usually in the warm upper layer, but will move into the thermocline if the upper layer becomes too warm.

NATURAL LAKES. Finding bass in summer is easier in natural lakes than in most reservoirs. Largemouths seldom have the selection of structure and cover available to reservoir bass. And they inhabit a narrow range of depths during summer.

The type of lake makes a difference when searching for bass in summer. Shallow, murky lakes have weedlines in 6 to 10 feet of water. Most bass stay along the weedline, but some move even shallower.

Deep, clear lakes have much deeper weedlines, usually from 15 to 20 feet. During midday, bass can be found along weedlines or on deep structure like sunken islands or points. They feed in the shallows in morning and evening.

Experts know that some bass stay in the shallows all day. There may be many more bass in deep water, but fish in shallow water are more likely to bite.

Southern marsh lakes generally have poor fishing once surface temperatures rise into the 80s. Bass cannot go deep because the depths lack oxygen or the basin is not deep enough to have any cooler water. Bass seek shade under the thickest overhead weed mass or on dense weedlines.

Finding bass in summer can be a challenge. Begin your search in the following hotspots:

•*Large docks* with canopies and many posts provide shade and cool water for bass. The best docks are near deep water and have weeds nearby.

•*Slop,* or thick overhead weeds, keeps the water cool and holds an abundant supply of food. Some bass can be found under slop all summer.

•*Rocky reefs* attract more bass than reefs with clean sand bottoms. Largemouths find shade among large rocks and boulders.

•*Weedlines* form where the water becomes too deep to allow enough light for weed growth. Look for bass along deep weedlines that have ragged edges.

•*Water-dwelling trees,* such as cypress, grow in many southern lakes and swamps. Look for bass around extensive root systems of the largest trees.

•*Points with irregular edges* and sharp drop-offs hold more largemouths than points with straight edges that drop off more gradually.

Reservoirs and Natural Lakes: Fall and Winter

RESERVOIRS. In early fall, cool temperatures coax bass up from the depths to begin their fall feeding spree. In flatland and cove reservoirs, bass cruise over large, timbered flats along creek channels. Deep junctions of creek channels are gathering points for bass filtering down both channels. Largemouths hang near points formed by the converging channels. They also roam shoals near shore and shallow points covered with brush and timber.

In canyon reservoirs, largemouths move into shallower arms where tributaries join the main body. Shallow points and gradually sloping rock slides will also hold fish.

After fall turnover, bass move much deeper and feed less frequently. The depth of bass in late fall varies from 25 feet in flatland reservoirs to 40 feet or deeper in cove and canyon reservoirs. Look for them along the steepest structure, in the bottoms of deep creek or river channels, in deep timber or along step-like ledges. They stay in these spots through winter. Sheer rock faces hold fewer bass.

Power companies use some reservoirs for drawing water to cool their turbines, then return the heated water to the lake. Called *cooling lakes*, these waters generally provide better fishing in late fall and winter than nearby lakes. The discharge warms the lake enough for bass to remain active. Cooling lakes in the South stay warm enough for anglers to catch bass anywhere in the lake. In the North, bass hang near the warm discharge because the rest of the lake is too cold.

NATURAL LAKES. Early fall finds bass patrolling shore-line flats covered with emergent vegetation such as bulrushes, or submerged plants like coontail or cabbage. Flats along protected shores warm faster and hold more largemouths than flats in mid-lake. Green weeds attract bass when most aquatic plants have died and turned brown. If you hook a piece of green vegetation, work the area thoroughly before moving. Docks, channels between lakes, and shallow points also hold bass.

Like fish in reservoirs, bass in natural lakes seek the steep-

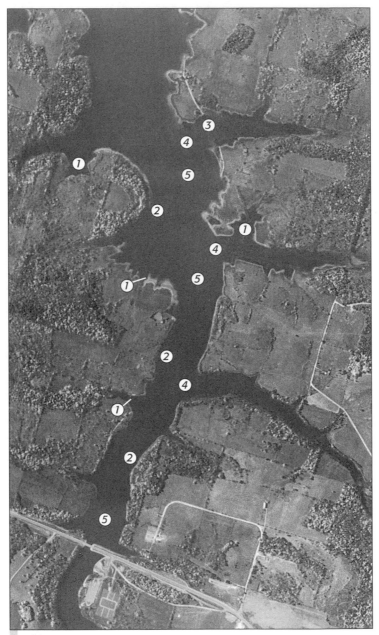

EARLY FALL LOCATIONS in reservoirs include: (1) shallow coves, (2) shorelines along the main body, (3) shallow areas of a road. Late fall and winter locations include: (4) deep intersections of creek channels and the main channel, (5) deep sections of the main channel.

est drop-offs in late fall. In bowl-shaped lakes, they move to the deepest holes they can find. Typical late fall depth varies from 20 to 40 feet, depending on water clarity. Bass swim shallower to feed on warm days, but as winter approaches, they form tighter schools, stay deep and feed very seldom.

In the Deep South, bass move in and out of deep wintering areas as the weather changes. A few days of warm temperatures draw them into shallow weedbeds to feed. Edges of hydrilla beds hold bass in natural lakes, especially if the weedline is along a drop-off. Bass may also inhabit sparse areas in the weeds. Fishing remains good until the next cold snap, when they retreat to deep water.

Shallow lakes provide the first good fishing in fall because they cool faster than deep lakes. But shallow lakes also turn over first, and bass move into their deep wintering spots earlier. As a result, a deeper lake is a better choice in late fall.

Rivers and Backwaters

Many bass fishermen overlook the nation's large river systems. Yet warmwater rivers offer excellent fishing for anglers who know where to find bass at different times of the year.

Dams on many large rivers have created fertile backwaters with sloughs, connecting lakes and side channels, or cuts. These quiet backwaters, with their flooded timber, brush and extensive weedbeds, provide good habitat for largemouths.

Bass spawn in shallow backwaters, then move toward deeper in the backwaters or nearby cuts. However, some may remain in weedy or brushy shallows through summer.

Largemouths are highly sensitive to falling water levels. If the level drops only a few inches in the backwaters, bass will move toward deeper water to avoid being trapped.

In northern rivers, bass usually remain in the backwaters through freeze-up. But as oxygen levels drop, they move to deeper areas in or near the main river channel. In southern regions where rivers do not freeze, largemouths may live in the backwaters year-round.

In rivers without backwaters, bass spawn on shallow sandbars with little or no current. After spawning they live near any features that break or deflect the current, such as logs, boulders and bridge pilings. Many largemouths school in deep pools and eddies along the main channel or just below large islands, points and sandbars. Undercut banks or rock ledges also attract bass.

Below are location tips for finding bass in rivers and backwaters:

•*Warmwater discharges* from power plants hold some bass from late fall to early spring. The fish wedge together in tight schools, usually at the edge of the warmwater plume.

•*Chutes* between islands off the main river channel concentrate bass foods. Look for deepwater chutes that empty into large pools.

BASS LOCATIONS include: (1) points along the main channel and (2) in the backwater lakes, (3) cuts leading into the backwaters, (4) riprap bank along a railroad embankment, (5) weedy shallows in the backwaters.

•*Bridges* offer shade and cover. Largemouths hold along the edges of abutments near shore and just above or below pilings in mid-stream.

•*Points* and the tips of islands draw feeding largemouths in morning and evening. Shaded points may hold bass throughout the day.

•*Riprap* along the main channel or in backwaters attracts minnows and crayfish. Bass feed among the jagged rocks, sometimes within inches of shore.

•*Stump fields* are spawning grounds for bass. Some largemouths will stay through summer if the water level does not drop below 2 feet.

•*Weedy shallows* attract spawning bass. The dense weeds shut out sunlight, keeping the water cool enough for bass through summer.

•*Fallen trees* and submerged logs in narrow cuts offer cover for largemouths. Cast along the shady side of these features.

Small Streams

To find bass in a small stream, you should know how to *read* the water. In clear streams, it is easy to see likely spots such as bars, boulders and sunken logs. But in murkier water, you must learn to identify current patterns that reveal the location of underwater structures.

RIFFLES hold feeding largemouths in early morning and just before dark. Bass rest behind a rock or log, then dart into swift water to grab food.

The best largemouth streams have slow to moderate current and warm water. Prime bass habitat includes eddies, deep pools and undercut banks.

An eddy is indicated by current flowing opposite from the main stream or debris floating in one spot. Bass move into quiet areas of eddies to escape the current. Look for an eddy downstream from an obstruction such as a point, fallen tree or boulder. A *surface boil* also reveals an eddy. A large, underwater object will deflect the current upward, creating a boil several feet downstream from the eddy.

A deep pool appears as an area of calm, dark water. Good pools have ample cover such as rocks, downed trees and sunken logs. Bass usually feed in shallow riffles or in the upstream part of a pool where current washes in food.

Undercut banks generally form along outside bends. Look for current flowing toward and disappearing under the stream bank. Tree roots, tall grasses or other stream bank vegetation hold the surface soil in place, creating a large overhang. Several bass may hide in the root tangle or just below the drooping grass. Bass also hide under rock ledges gouged out by the current.

Dams block largemouths moving upstream to find a spawning area. Look for bass in slack water on both sides of the main stream.

Bass often spend their entire lives in a small section of stream. In spring, they may swim only a few yards upstream to find shallow gravel bars suitable for spawning. In winter, bass hold in the deepest pools.

Estuaries

Few anglers would ever dream of catching a saltwater gamefish one minute and a largemouth bass the next. But it happens in many coastal estuaries.

A coastal river flowing into the sea creates an estuary. The fresh and salt water mix to make brackish water. An estuary extends upstream to a point where higher land elevation prevents the sea water from advancing any farther. The salt water may penetrate 100 miles inland where large rivers flow across flat terrain. On rivers that drop quickly from high elevation, the estuary is much shorter.

Estuaries offer a variety of bass habitat including bays, islands and deep channels. The lower end may be too salty, except for bays fed by freshwater tributaries.

Estuaries are generally narrow at their upper end, but widen near the ocean. The lower end may be an intricate maze of deep channels cutting through a shallow flat. Or it may resemble a large lake or river backwater. Some estuaries have adjoining brackish marshes that are also connected to the sea.

Largemouths in brackish water may be found in the same vicinity as ocean fish such as snook and tarpon. The bass commonly feed on saltwater baitfish like herring, and various kinds of shellfish, particularly shrimp and crabs.

Tidal currents dictate bass movement in estuaries. Tides change the current direction every 6 to 12 hours. Water levels normally fluctuate several feet, but fluctuations vary from only a few inches to more than 10 feet. Bass move to find slack-water areas and to feed on baitfish and shellfish that are also adjusting to the changing current and water level. During low tide, bass often concentrate in deeper pools and cuts.

One of the best times to fish is during *high slack*, the brief, stable-water period following the peak of a high tide. Fishing is also good at *low slack*, the stable-water period following low tide. Check the tide table in a local newspaper for the times of high and low tides.

Locating bass in the narrow, upper part of an estuary is similar to locating bass in a slow-moving river. Look for them along steep banks, in eddies or where small tributaries enter the main channel. Bass in the lower portion are caught on large, weedy flats or in dense weedbeds bordering deep channels. The best cover is always under water, even at low tide.

Ponds

Many fishermen think that small ponds produce only small fish. But several state-record bass, including a 14-pound, 4-ounce Alabama largemouth, have been caught in ponds.

Landowners build ponds either by damming a small creek or dry wash, or by bulldozing a basin in a low-lying area. Most farm ponds are stocked with largemouths and sunfish.

Ponds in the North can support bass if most of the water is 15 feet or deeper. Shallow ponds winter-kill. In the South, ponds only a few feet deep produce bass.

The best ponds have light to moderate weed growth. If vegetation is too dense, bass populations decline. In light weeds, bass keep the number of sunfish in check. But if weeds are heavy, too many sunfish escape and their population skyrockets. The hungry sunfish quickly wipe out bass nests.

Fishing is best in spring. Ponds warm faster than nearby lakes, so angling may begin several weeks earlier. Look for bass in shallow, weedy areas near the inflow end or where shoreline grasses droop over the water.

Angling success usually tapers off in summer, especially in shallow ponds, which offer no refuge from warm surface temperatures. Bass become lethargic and difficult to catch. Deeper ponds form thermoclines during summer so bass can retreat to the depths to find cooler water. However, they feed in weedy shallows in morning and evening.

Pond-fishing improves in fall as bass return to the shallows. In late fall, bass edge toward the deepest areas of the pond where they find the warmest water. They remain deep through winter.

Except during the spring spawning season, some bass can always be found near fish attractors in deep water. If possible, ask the landowner to point out the approximate location of any attractors. These are big-bass hotspots that probably receive little fishing pressure.

Pits and Quarries

Most people consider abandoned mine pits to be eyesores. But to a savvy bass angler, an abandoned pit offers a fishing opportunity often overlooked by the masses.

Coal strip mines, or *strip pits*, are found in many eastern states, but primarily in Ohio, Illinois, Indiana and Kentucky. Old pits are seldom deeper than 20 feet; newer pits may be 100 feet deep.

Pits with a maximum depth of about 40 feet offer the best fishing. Deeper pits produce fewer bass because their waters are cold and infertile. In many old pits, the water is too acidic to support fish.

Recent reclamation laws are reducing the amount of acid runoff into pits, making it possible for newly stocked bass to survive. If you are unsure whether a strip pit has fish, check the shoreline for minnows or other small baitfish. If you fail to see any, the water is probably too acidic.

Fishermen also catch largemouths in gravel, iron-ore and phosphate pits. Gravel pits throughout the country have been stocked with largemouths, especially in the Plains States. Minnesota has hundreds of abandoned iron-ore pits that offer excellent fishing. Phosphate pits in central Florida produce large numbers of trophy bass.

Most easy-to-reach pits offer fair fishing, while inaccessible basins often teem with bass. If the pit has infertile water, even moderate fishing pressure will quickly reduce its bass population.

Cover is the key to finding bass in pits. Look for fallen trees, logs, brush and rock slides. The best bass locations in deep pits include: spawning sites on rocks or gravel; summer holding areas on mid-depth ledges, but close to shallow water; early fall feeding areas in the shallows; wintering sites next to sheer walls in deep water.

STRIP PITS usually have crystal-clear waters. Most are long and narrow with one steep edge and one gradually sloping shore. The ends are usually shallow.

Weather & Bass Location

Weather plays a greater role in the daily activity of largemouth bass than any other factor. To improve your success, you should know how the following weather conditions affect bass fishing.

STABLE WEATHER. When weather conditions are stable or gradually changing, bass go through a routine of feed-

ing and resting that is often predictable from one day to the next. For example, during an extended period of overcast weather, a school of bass may feed on a sharp-breaking point at midday, then drop back into deeper water. The school usually repeats this daily pattern, as long as weather conditions remain stable.

FRONTS. Largemouths feed heavily just before a strong cold front, often providing spectacular fishing for several hours. But once the front arrives, they eat very little until 1 or 2 days after the system passes. Catching bass under these conditions is difficult and requires special techniques with lighter lines and smaller lures. A cold front affects bass fishing in the following manner:

•*Cirrus clouds* usually precede a major cold front. These clouds may be 100 miles ahead of an approaching front. They indicate that largemouths will soon be feeding heavily.

•*Thunderheads* build as a front approaches. Lightning and strong winds often accompany these towering clouds. The feeding frenzy may peak just before these clouds arrive.

•*Stalled fronts* may leave skies overcast for several days. Look for bass feeding in the shallows during this low-light condition.

•*Clear sky* following a cold front filters out few of the sun's rays. Light penetrates deeper into the water, forcing bass to move out of the shallows.

•*Cumulus clouds* promise better fishing. The white, fluffy clouds signal that the cold front has passed. Bass will soon resume their normal activity.

Warm fronts affect bass in different ways, depending on the season and water temperatures. A series of warm days in spring or fall will raise water temperatures in the shallows, causing bass to feed.

In winter, several unusually warm days may draw bass toward the surface to absorb the warmth of the sun. The fish become more accessible to fishermen and more likely to feed or take a lure. But a string of hot days in summer may warm a shallow lake or pond so much that largemouths become sluggish and difficult to catch.

WIND. Like warming trends, wind can either improve or ruin fishing. A steady wind will concentrate minute organisms near shore or along timber and brush lines. Baitfish feed in these areas, attracting bass and other predators. In spring, warm winds blowing from the same direction for several days can pile up warm water on the downwind shore. This warmer water holds more bass than other areas of the lake.

Waves washing into shore loosen soil and debris, creating a band of muddy water. Bass hang along the *mud line,* where they can avoid bright light, but still dart into clear water to grab food.

If the wind becomes too strong, it can impair fishing success in shallow areas. Turbulence caused by heavy waves pushes bass into deeper water, where they are harder to find. In shallow lakes, strong winds often churn the water enough to make the entire lake murky, slowing fishing for several days.

Calm conditions enable bass in clear water to see objects above them. Fishermen and boaters easily spook bass in shallow water. Wave action bends or refracts light rays, making it more difficult for largemouths to see movements on or above the surface.

RAIN. Rainy weather usually improves bass fishing. The overcast skies reduce light penetration, so bass are more comfortable in shallow water. In reservoirs, runoff flows into the back ends of coves. The murky water causes bass to move in and feed. The same situation occurs near stream inlets, drainage ditches or storm sewer pipes on many natural lakes.

Fishing success may decline during and after heavy rains. Runoff from torrential rains can muddy an entire body of water, causing fish to stop biting. Angling remains slow until the water clears, which may take several days or weeks.

Lightning and thunder drive largemouths into the depths. If the weather looks threatening, you should head for shore immediately. Your boat may be the highest point on the lake, making you vulnerable to a lightning strike.

Experienced fishermen can identify certain clouds and other atmospheric conditions that indicate coming changes in the weather. They know how bass react to these changes and plan their angling strategy accordingly.

BASS-FISHING
EQUIPMENT

Bass Boats

The evolution of the bass boat can be traced to the sprawling reservoirs of the South. Bass fishermen wanted a boat that could be operated at high speeds, so they could travel to distant fishing spots in a hurry. They needed a boat that could be maneuvered through thick weedbeds and stump fields in shallow water. They also wanted a stable, comfortable craft with a raised casting deck.

Fiberglass bass boats are the number-one choice of bass anglers throughout the country. These rigs, which often cost between $15,000 and $30,000, give anglers a comfort-

able, dry ride even in rough water. Boats with high-performance hulls are powered by 75- to 250-hp engines. Some can easily exceed 65 mph.

Aluminum bass boats are lighter and less expensive than most fiberglass models. They can be launched easily, even at shallow, unimproved sites. Most aluminum boats have 30- to 115-hp outboard motors. These boats are becoming more popular because they are less expensive to buy and operate than fiberglass models.

An ignition kill switch is an important safety feature on

high-speed boats. The switch is attached to the boat operator and the engine's ignition. If the angler is thrown from his seat, the engine shuts off.

A modern, fully equipped bass boat is the ultimate fishing machine, offering many features intended to help you find and catch more fish, and enabling you to fish in comfort.

Most top-of-the-line fiberglass bass boats have the following features: padded chairs, battery and equipment storage areas, console-mounted depth finder, large rod-storage compartments, bow-mounted depth finder, electric trolling motor, temperature gauge, compass, GPS (Global Positioning System), speedometer, automatic bilge pump, electric anchor, marine radio, weather radio, tape deck, special lights for night fishing, large-capacity gas tank, air-ride pedestal "bike seats" on elevated casting decks, built-in cooler, and live well with a timer and recirculating pump. Some boats even have a built-in charging system, so you can charge batteries more easily.

Perhaps the most important feature on any bass boat is its electric trolling motor. These motors allow pinpoint boat control. You can choose from foot-control or hand-control models. Foot controls on bow-mounted electric trolling motors enable you to change boat speed and direction, leaving your hands free to cast or fight a fish. Select a motor with at least 48 pounds of thrust. A motor with pulse-width modulation greatly conserves battery life, particularly at low motor speeds. Be sure the motor you choose has a weedless prop.

But many veteran bass fishermen prefer to keep their boat rigging very simple, using only a depth finder and an electric trolling motor. They maintain that the more equipment you have, the more time you spend in the repair shop.

Small Boats & Inflatables

You do not need an expensive boat to catch bass. Fishermen pursue largemouths in float tubes, inflatable boats, canoes, jon boats and a variety of small craft designed for cartop racks or light trailers.

Small boats and float tubes are perfect for isolated lakes, small ponds and other waters where launching a big boat would be impossible. And as many bass anglers know, these hard-to-reach waters frequently offer prime bass fishing, sometimes within minutes of heavily populated areas.

When fishing far from a road, some anglers strap on a float tube and walk to the water. Float tubes strap on the angler's shoulders. Be sure the canvas seat has a quick-release mechanism, so you can slide out if the tube flips over. Most tubes have an inside diameter of 16 to 20 inches. The larger sizes provide more stability. Fishermen can attach kick fins to their waders for propelling the tube forward. Some anglers wear swimming trunks, then use standard swim fins and push the tube backward. Tubes should not be used in heavy waves or strong current. For safety, anglers work in pairs.

The best inflatable boats are made from puncture-resistant, heavy-gauge vinyl with nylon backing. They have several air compartments, so if one is punctured, the boat will still float. Features on most inflatable fishing boats include tackle-storage compartments, inflatable seats, oarlocks and

CANOES (top, left), small aluminum boats (top, right) and float tubes (right) enable smart anglers to cash in on trophy fisheries not reachable by anglers with large bass boats.

wood transoms for attaching gas or electric motors. Models used for bass fishing are usually rigged with 2- to 4-hp outboards, but some boats can be outfitted with motors up to 25 hp. Transport an inflated boat on a cartop carrier. A deflated or partially inflated boat can be hauled in a station wagon. Controlling an inflatable can be difficult in wind, so bring along an anchor.

Small, molded plastic boats can also be loaded into a station wagon. They range from 70 to about 100 pounds and 7 to 10 feet in length. They should be used only on quiet waters. Molded plastic boats come in one- and two-man models. Most have built-in lure trays, rod racks and removable swivel chairs.

Canoes work best on quiet lakes and ponds and on small streams. They are ideal for portaging from one body of water to another. Canoes are lightweight but they tip easily, especially when the angler is fighting and landing a fish. For extra stability, lash a long board or pole across the canoe, then attach a large Styrofoam float.

Jon boats offer good side-to-side stability because of their flat bottoms. Jon boats with a semi-V bow work best for cutting through waves. Flat-bottom jon boats draw only a few inches of water. They work well in stump fields or shallow, rocky rivers. The blunt bow and low sides of a jon boat make it a poor choice in rough water.

Some anglers rig small boats with gas or electric motors, depth finders, swivel seats and many of the accessories used on larger craft. Most tube fishermen carry only a pocket-sized lure box, one rod and a rope stringer.

Depth Finders

A depth finder may well be your most important fishing tool, because it enables you to locate likely bass habitat in minutes.

All depth finders have a transducer that emits a sonar signal, and a receiver that converts the returning signal to a display of the bottom, fish, weeds or other objects.

Common types of depth finders include liquid-crystal recorders (LCRs), videos and flashers.

LIQUID-CRYSTALS. These are the most popular of all depth finders. They're compact and fairly inexpensive, yet they clearly show the bottom and the fish.

Liquid-crystal recorders should have at least 128 vertical pixels to provide adequate detail; some units have 200 or more. Some units also have a digital depth readout and "zoom" capability, allowing you to select a specific depth range out of the water column.

Some liquid-crystals provide a 3-D readout; others, called "sidefinders," enable you to see what's off to the side of the boat. But many anglers question the reliability of these units, maintaining that they often give misleading signals.

VIDEOS. Available in 8-color or monochrome models, videos display signals on a cathode-ray tube, similar to

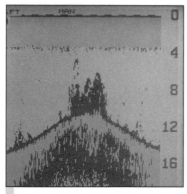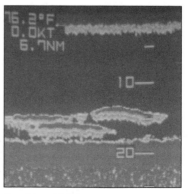

Liquid-crystal recorder (left) and color video (right)

that in a television set. They're bulkier and more expensive than most other types of depth finders, but provide excellent detail.

Color videos show fish in different colors, giving you an idea of their relative size. Red marks indicate large fish; lighter-color marks, smaller fish. Some units also have digital depth and zoom features, and show surface temperature, speed and distance traveled.

FLASHERS. These units display the bottom, fish and other objects as red blips on a circular, calibrated dial. Some flashers even display different-sized objects in different colors. A flasher with a 0- to 30-foot scale is the best choice for bass fishing. Units with greater-depth scales show less detail. Because of the popularity of  LCRs, however, some major manufacturers have discontinued flashers.

When you purchase a depth finder, read through the owner's manual to learn how to use it properly. Nothing will help you catch more fish than a thorough understanding of what you're viewing on your electronics. The most important underwater objects to look for include:

•*Drop-offs*, or breaklines, appear as a sloping band on a graph. On a flasher, sharp drop-offs appear as wide bands.

•*Weeds* appear as black clumps above a clearly defined bottom on a graph. A flasher indicates weeds by thin blips above the bottom signal.

•*Flooded timber* shows up as solid, heavy tracings above bottom on a graph. On a flasher, the trees appear as thick flashes above the bottom reading.

•*Suspended bass* form a cluster of inverted V shapes on a graph. A flasher shows a series of blips. On both units, thicker signals generally indicate larger fish.

Maps

Only a small fraction of the water in any lake contains largemouth bass. A good *hydrographic,* or contour map, used with a depth finder, can save hours of random searching.

Hydrographic maps indicate water depth by contour lines. Maps usually show a contour line at every 5- or 10-foot depth change. Lines that are close together reveal abrupt bottom changes; lines far apart mean a gradually sloping bottom.

Maps show the location of good bass-holding structure such as sunken islands, creek channels and submerged points. Maps of reservoirs sometimes pinpoint man-made features that have been flooded, including roads and houses. Most maps show various shoreline features, while some identify bottom types and the locations of weedbeds,

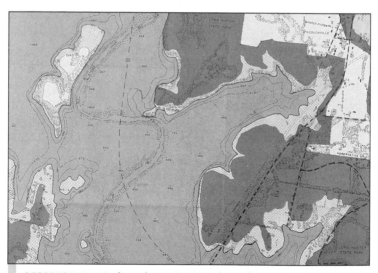

RESERVOIR MAPS show the main river channel, points, islands, road and powerline crossings, and contour lines. Mileage from the dam is shown along the river channel and the shortest navigable route. Red indicates a state park, dots are flooded trees and X's show elevations at selected locations.

flooded timber and brush.

After studying your contour map, look for a landmark such as a point to help you find the right vicinity. Then use your depth finder to locate the exact spot. If you catch fish, mark the spot on your map. Before leaving, check the shoreline for reference points, then list them on your map. The spot will be easier to find next time.

Contour maps of natural lakes seldom show every detail on bottom. Mapmakers often miss humps and reefs. These small structures may lie between survey lines used by crews when charting lake depths.

It pays to do some extra scouting and pencil in any features that the map does not show. Few fishermen discover these areas, so they sometimes offer prime fishing.

Hydrographic maps are available for most natural lakes and reservoirs. To purchase these maps, contact your state fish and wildlife agency, the U.S. Army Corps of Engineers, the Tennessee Valley Authority, or private map publishers. Power companies sometimes supply maps of their cooling lakes.

LAKE MAPS identify many features including: points, sunken islands where the shallowest depth is in the center, distinct breaklines, deep holes where the maximum depth is in the center, islands, public boat ramps, and submerged points. Hills and steep banks on this map could be used as reference points.

Rods, Reels & Line

When selecting rods, reels and line for bass fishing, check manufacturer's recommendations. Don't try to pair a rod recommended for 6- to 8-pound mono with a reel recommended for 10- to 15-pound. A heavy reel would impair the outfit's balance and sensitivity.

Following are important considerations in rod, reel and line selection:

RODS. Most bass rods are relatively stiff, for strong hook sets and good sensitivity. And the stiffness comes in handy for horsing fish out of heavy cover.

Baitcasting rods generally range from 5½ to 7 feet in length, with power designations from medium-light to extra-heavy. Most spinning rods are 5½ to 7 feet long and range from light to medium-heavy. Fly rods vary from 8 to 9½ feet and carry line-weight designations from 8 to 10.

Many bass anglers also carry several different types of special-purpose rods.

•*Flippin' rods* are about 7½ feet long, usually heavy power, and have a telescopic design for easy storage. The extra length enables you to flip lures into hard-to-reach spots, and comes in handy for other uses, such as casting crankbaits and slowly retrieving buzz baits.

•*Pitchin' rods*, usually 6½ feet long, are medium-heavy in power with a fast action. *Pitchin'* means tossing lures under low cover, such as branches or docks, using an underhand, low-trajectory, swing cast. When pitched properly, the lure travels only a few inches above the water.

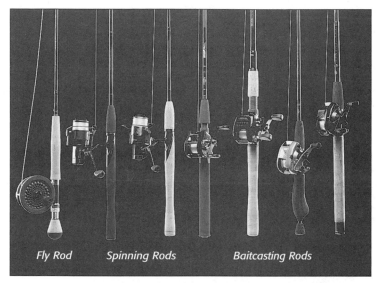

Fly Rod   Spinning Rods   Baitcasting Rods

RODS AND REELS commonly used for largemouths include fly rods, for casting large bass flies; spinning rods, for casting light lures and skipping lures under cover; and baitcasting rods, for jigging, pitchin', crankin' and flippin'.

•*Crankin' rods* are 6½ to 7 feet long with medium power. They have a slow action because of their fiberglass construction. They're intended to hold hooked fish better than stiffer rods; when the fish thrashes, the rod bends instead of the hooks tearing out. Crankin' rods work best with crankbaits, buzz baits or topwater plugs, because little sensitivity is needed to detect strikes.

With the exception of crankin' rods and some specialty trolling rods, most quality bass rods are made of light-weight, sensitive graphite.

Before purchasing a bass rod of any type, inspect its line guides. Quality rods have more guides than cheap rods. Also look for rods with silicone carbide or aluminum oxide guides. While these guides are slightly more expensive, they cause less line damage than those made from other materials.

REELS. Most baitcasting reels have a push button or thumb bar that switches the reel to free spool. This eliminates resistance that would result from a turning reel handle, allowing longer casts. Some top-quality reels have a magnetic anti-backlash device that places slight pressure on the spool to prevent overruns. You can adjust the anti-backlash mechanism on a free-spool casting reel by tightening or loosening the knob. The lure should fall slowly when the reel is in free-spool. This device is superior to mechanisms that operate by friction. But fishermen must still thumb the spool to prevent backlashes.

A narrow-spool reel is less likely to backlash because the light spool does not have as much momentum. This type of reel is recommended for pitchin', because anglers using this technique often keep the spool tension loose so the cast does not stop short of the target.

Spinning reels should have interchangeable spools so you can change line quickly. A longer-than-normal spool adds distance to your casts and, because it holds more line, allows you to cast well even when a fair amount of the line has been lost.

Consider the gear ratio when choosing any reel. A high-speed reel has a ratio of 5:1 to 7:1, enabling faster retrieves for rapid-fire casting. Reels with ball bearings operate more smoothly and last longer than those with bushings.

Be sure to test the drag before purchasing any reel. Wind on some line, then pull it off at different drag settings. A sticky drag means a snapped line, should you hook a big bass.

Practically any fly reel will work for bass fishing. Fly reels are mainly for line storage, so there's no need to buy an expensive model.

LINE. Almost all bass fishermen us monofilament line. Use the lightest mono practical for the conditions. Light line casts better, allows more lure action and is less visible to fish. You can also choose one of the new thin-diameter braided or fused "superlines." These lines are incredibly strong and have no stretch. Use abrasion-resistant mono or one of the superlines when fishing around rocks, weeds, timber or brush. Use soft, limp mono when fishing in unobstructed water.

Medium-power, general-purpose baitcasting gear is usually wound with 10- to 17-pound line; heavy baitcasting gear used in dense cover, 20- to 30-pound. Light spinning gear requires 6- to 8-pound line; medium spinning gear, 8- to 12-pound.

Most fly fishermen use weight-forward line to overcome the weight and wind resistance of large bugs and poppers, and for punching into a wind.

KNOTS. Regardless of your line choice, you need to tie good knots to successfully hook and land bass. The easiest knot to tie is the Trilene Knot. It retains about 90 percent of the line's originally rated strength. When you want a lure to swing freely on a loop for maximum action, tie a Duncan Loop, which also retains 90 percent of the line's strength.

Trilene Knot

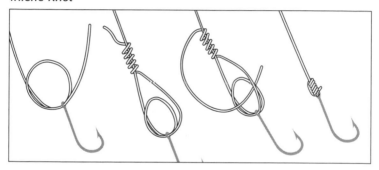

Duncan Loop

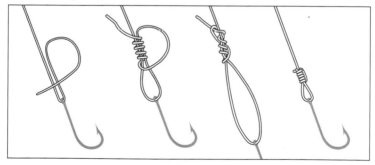

Soft Plastics

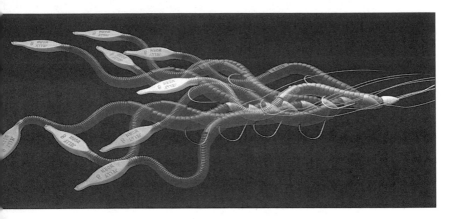

When asked to choose their favorite lure, the majority of anglers at a national bass-fishing championship named the plastic worm. The lure is effective because of its tantalizing, lifelike action. And when inhaled by a bass, the worm's soft body feels like natural food.

Plastic worms and other soft plastics work best in warm water. You can retrieve them through thick weeds or brush without snagging, float them over shallow cover or jig them along deep structure. Generally, soft plastics are not as effective in cold water.

Some soft plastics resemble crayfish, eels, salamanders, lizards or even small snakes. Others look like nothing a bass has ever seen.

Plastic worms range from 4 to 12 inches. The 6- to 18-inch sizes work best in most situations. Use smaller worms in clear water or when bass nip at a lure, such as after a cold front. Some anglers crawl 12-inch, snakelike worms over heavy cover to catch trophy bass.

Experiment to find the best color. Purple and black soft plastics will catch bass in almost any type of water. In murky water, solid, gaudy colors such as chartreuse or red may work better. Many soft plastics have bright or fluorescent tails, called *firetails*, or metal flakes molded into the body for extra attraction in murky water. In very clear water, try translucent plastics in soft colors such as blue, grape or red.

When fishing in heavy cover, rig a soft plastic Texas-style (p. 68). Most fishermen use cone-shaped slip-sinkers. For better feel when fishing in brush or timber, some anglers peg the sinker to the line. Use a 1/16- or 1/8-ounce sinker in water less than 6 feet deep, 1/8- or 1/4-ounce in 6 to 12 feet, 1/4- or 3/8-ounce in 13 to 18 feet and 3/8- or 1/2-ounce in water deeper than 18 feet.

To rig a soft plastic for surface fishing, use a plain hook and no sinker. If the lure sinks, cut small slits in the body and insert bits of Styrofoam. Some manufacturers offer soft plastics with extra floatation.

Where snags are not a problem, some anglers thread a plastic worm onto a plain jig head or use a Carolina rig (below).

For best results, rig plastic worms on large, long-shank hooks. Many worm hooks have barbs to keep the worm from sliding down the shank. If the shank does not have barbs, slide the worm over the eye of the hook and anchor it by pushing a toothpick through the worm and eye. Trim off the ends of the toothpick.

Hook size depends mainly on the size of the worm. Use a #1 or 1/0 hook with a 4-inch worm, a 2/0 or 3/0 with a 6-inch worm, a 4/0 or 5/0 with an 8-inch worm and a 5/0 or 6/0 with a 10-inch worm.

Fishing with soft plastics demands a delicate touch. A strike, or pickup, usually feels like a light tap. But

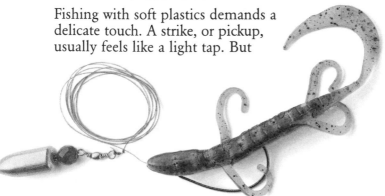

sometimes the line moves off to one side or the lure suddenly feels weightless. Bass take soft plastics with a quick gulp. If you feel anything unusual, set the hook.

Use a rod heavy enough to drive the hook into the tough jaw of a bass, yet sensitive enough to detect a subtle strike. A powerful hook set places considerable stress on the line. Check it periodically to make sure it is free of nicks. Tie the line directly to the hook with a secure knot, rather than attaching it with a clip or snap-swivel.

HOW TO RIG A PLASTIC WORM TEXAS-STYLE

THREAD the line through a sliding cone sinker and tie on a plastic-worm hook. Insert the point about 1/2 inch into the worm's head.

PUSH the point through and slide the worm up the shank to cover the eye. Rotate the hook one-half turn and bury the point in the worm.

AVOID twisting the plastic worm before inserting the hook. If it does not hang straight, the worm will revolve and twist the line as it is retrieved.

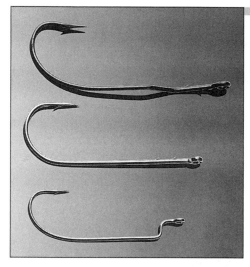

POPULAR HOOKS for rigging soft plastics include: Tru-Turn Cam Action (top), which rotates on the hook set; Owner straight shank with barbs (middle); Owner light-wire offset (bottom), for fishing small worms.

Most anglers who have trouble catching bass with soft plastics fish the lures too fast. The following describes how to fish a Texas-rigged plastic worm in most situations:

•*Cast,* then hold the rod tip high as the worm settles. Allow enough slack so the lure can sink, but keep enough tension so you can detect a strike. Bass often take a worm as it sinks.

•*Crawl* the worm across the bottom about 1 foot by raising your rod tip. Pause and watch your line for a twitch, which indicates a strike. Lower your rod tip and wind in 1 foot of line without moving the lure. Raise the rod tip and crawl the worm another foot to repeat the process.

•*Drop* the rod tip when you detect a pickup. Lean forward and point the rod at the fish. The bass should not feel any resistance at this crucial point.

•*Set the hook* immediately with a powerful upward sweep of the rod. Jerk hard enough so the hook penetrates the worm and the bass's jaw. If the first hook set does not feel solid, set the hook again.

•*Keep the rod tip high* and the line tight. The bass will lunge for cover the moment it feels the hook. Maintain steady pressure so the fish cannot wrap the line around weeds or brush.

Spinnerbaits

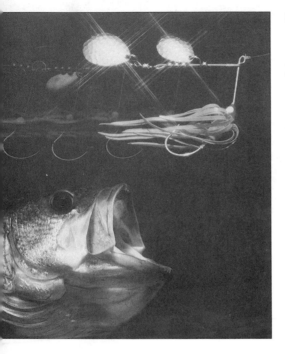

The outstanding success of the spinnerbait proves that a lure does not have to imitate natural bass food. A spinnerbait attracts bass with its flash, action and color. These qualities, combined with its semi-snagless design, make it a favorite among anglers who fish weedy or brushy waters.

The spinnerbait combines two excellent lures, the spinner and the jig. The wire shaft resembles an open safety pin. It has a lead-head jig on the lower arm and one or two spinners on the upper arm. Models with one blade are called *single-spins* (opposite page); those with a pair of blades are called *tandem* spinnerbaits. The best spinnerbaits have ball-bearing swivels so the blades can turn rapidly. Most models have a plastic or rubber skirt that adds action and conceals the hook.

Many anglers customize their spinnerbaits to change the action or color. Carry a variety of skirts and blades, and keep switching until you find the combination that works best. You can change blades easily if the spinnerbait has a snap-swivel on the upper arm. However, blades are not always interchangeable. A blade that is too large will cause the entire lure to revolve. Some manufacturers make spinnerbaits with straight skirts, but most anglers reverse the skirt for better action.

To increase the hooking percentage on spinnerbaits you can add a trailer hook. Because a trailer hook stays in line with the forward hook and wire shaft the lure remains weedless.

You can also clamp on a split-shot, lead wire or pinch-on sinker to the lower arm of a spinnerbait to reach bass in deeper water. The weighted spinnerbait will sink faster, causing the blades to helicopter rapidly.

Spinnerbaits can be retrieved many different ways. Experiment to find the best retrieve for the situation at hand. The following are the three most popular spinnerbait retrieves:

•*Steady retrieve.* Reel a spinnerbait through weeds or brush, varying the speed and depth on successive retrieves. The hook lies directly behind the wire arms, which keep the hook from fouling in weeds.

•*Buzz retrieve.* Begin reeling a tandem-blade spinnerbait as soon as it hits the water. Keep the rod tip high and reel rapidly so the top blade barely breaks the surface. Try this retrieve in warm shallows over heavy cover.

•*Life-and-drop retrieve.* Cast a spinnerbait, then let it slowly helicopter to the bottom. Raise your rod to lift the lure, reel in slack, lower your rod so the lure helicopters back to the bottom, then repeat.

Whenever possible, rap a spinnerbait against submerged brush, stumps or timber to give it an erratic action. Some anglers cast the lure past a visible obstruction such as a bridge piling or dock post, then retrieve to intentionally hit the object. The sudden change in the lure's speed and direction may trigger an immediate strike.

If a spinnerbait doesn't run with the blade directly above the hook, you can tune it by bending the upper arm to align with the hook. A properly tuned spinnerbait runs with its blades on top.

Subsurface Plugs

Even the most stubborn largemouth finds it difficult
to resist a plug wiggling enticingly past its nose. Plugs
work well for locating bass because you can cover a
lot of water quickly.

Bass anglers use three basic styles of subsurface plugs:
crankbaits, minnow plugs and vibrating plugs. Most plugs
are made of plastic, either hard or foamed, or wood, usually balsa or cedar. Some plugs have rattle chambers filled
with metal beads that create extra noise and vibration.

Although color selection changes from day to day, bright-colored plugs tend to work best in murky water, dull- or natural-colored plugs in clear water. Subsurface plugs often mimic crayfish or baitfish. Some manufacturers use a photographic process to give their plugs a lifelike appearance. Most anglers prefer plugs from 2 to 4 inches long for largemouths.

Crankbaits (right) have a comparatively short, wide body and a violent wobble. The length, width and angle of the lip determines the running depth. Some models with long, wide lips that extend straight off the nose can reach depths of 20 feet. Most crankbaits float at rest, but some sink, so you can count them down.

Minnow plugs are longer and slimmer than crankbaits and generally have a smaller lip, resulting in a gentler, but more lifelike, action. They come in floating and sinking models, as well as jointed and straight models. Floaters can be worked on the surface with a twitch-and-pause retrieve or reeled steadily to run at depths of 1 to 5 feet. Some long-lipped floaters dive to a depth of 12 feet. Sinking models can be counted down to any depth.

Vibrating plugs have a deep, narrow body, an attachment eye on the back and no lip. They have a tight wiggle that gives off high-frequency sound waves detectable by fish even in murky water. Most vibrating plugs sink, so you can fish them at any depth.

All subsurface plugs should be fished with the lightest line practical for the conditions. You'll cast farther and the plug will run deeper because there is less water resistance on the line.

For maximum wobble, attach a plug to your line with a split-ring or snap, not a heavy snap-swivel. Or, tie on the lure with a loop knot. Snugging the knot directly to the attachment eye may restrict the lure's action, particularly when you're using heavy line.

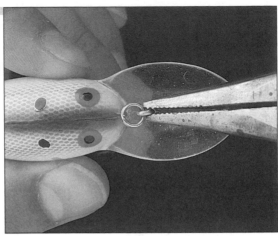

TUNE the lure by adjusting the angle of the eye. If the crankbait is tracking to the right, turn or bend the eye to the left.

Always experiment with different retrieve speeds. As a rule, the warmer the water, the faster the retrieve you should use. Often, an erratic stop-and-go retrieve will catch more bass than a steady retrieve.

Begin your stop-and-go retrieve by reeling rapidly to pull a floating-diving crankbait below the surface. Continue reeling to draw the lure deeper, then stop momentarily to let it rise. Continue to reel, using the stop-and-go technique. This retrieve is effective when the water is warm and largemouths are active. Another trick: give the plug an occasional twitch as you reel. The change in action sometimes triggers fish that aren't feeding.

Surface Lures

O ne of the most exciting moments in fishing is just after your surface lure hits the water. As the ripples die, you can almost sense the bass eyeing your lure. You know that the surface may erupt at any second.

Surface, or *topwater*, lures work best on calm summer mornings and evenings when bass are feeding in the shallows. They are not as effective in water below 60°F or when the surface is rough.

Topwater lures may be the only solution for catching bass nestled under thick mats of vegetation. The commotion often attracts bass even though they cannot see the lure. In this type of cover, anglers sometimes catch bass during midday.

Surface lures also work well for night fishing. Bass may not be able to see a deep-running lure. But they can detect the noise and vibration of a topwater lure. And when they move closer, they can see its silhouette against the moonlit sky.

Bass anglers use seven basic types of topwater lures:

PROPELLER-TYPE PLUGS have a long, thin body with a small propeller at one or both ends. Cast the lure, then wait for the ripples to die. Leave enough slack so the lure does not move forward. Twitch the rod tip slightly so the lure barely moves. Twitching against a slack line produces a sharper jerk. Blades spin as the lure darts forward. Wait for a few seconds, then twitch the lure again. Before buying a propeller-type plug, blow on the blades to make sure they turn freely.

POPPERS AND CHUGGERS (below) have a concave face that creates a popping or gurgling sound when retrieved. Most models have a rubber or plastic skirt. To fish these lures, make a long cast and wait for the ripples to subside after it hits the water. Sometimes bass will strike as the lure bobs on the surface or while it is motionless. Jerk the lure so it pops or chugs across the water. Lower the rod tip and keep the line tight, so you can set the hook the instant a fish strikes.

BUZZ BAITS resemble spinnerbaits, but the blade revolves around a shaft rather than spinning on a swivel. The large aluminum blade generates turbulence as the lure churns across the surface. Some models have tandem blades. The most popular retrieve is to rip a buzz bait across the surface. Its winged blade will churn the water, leaving a wake of bubbles. To make the lure noisier, bend the top arm so the blade clacks against either the shaft or lead head.

TOPWATER CRAWLERS have a metal lip or arms that cause the lure to wobble widely from side to side. Most crawlers make a loud, gurgling sound when retrieved. To get the most action from these lures you should jerk them across the surface by twitching the rod tip as you reel steady. Or reel a short distance, then stop while you twitch the lure. Topwater crawlers are especially effective at night.

STICKBAITS resemble propeller-type plugs, but they lack propellers. Anglers must twitch the lure to give it action. To walk a stickbait across the surface you need to reel slowly while twitching the rod tip. This type of retrieve is widely used by fishermen on southern reservoirs to bring largemouths up from deep water.

SURFACE WOBBLERS may look like a spoon or a lead-head jig with a large, upturned metal lip. They have plastic or rubber skirts to disguise the hook. Most have weedguards so they can be skittered across shallow weeds without fouling. You can skim a lightweight plastic weedless spoon across the surface by keeping your rod tip high as you reel. Or, retrieve with a twitching motion. You can draw these lures over dense weeds and brush without snagging or fouling.

ARTIFICIAL FROGS AND RATS have weedless hooks and can be retrieved over thick slop without fouling. These soft rubber or plastic-bodied lures work best when you twitch them at a quick pace through lily pads and other emergent vegetation. Bass usually strike when the lure moves into a pocket.

Bass will sometimes follow surface lures repeatedly without striking. You may be able to see the wake just behind the lure. To coax a strike, stop reeling, let the lure rest for several seconds, then twitch it. Not every bass strikes with an explosive smash. Sometimes a strike is merely a gentle slurp. Set the hook when you feel the weight of the fish on the end of the line.

Jigs & Jigging Lures

Bass that ignore fast-running plugs will often strike lures jigged vertically near their hiding spots. Jigging lures, including lead-head jigs, jigging spoons, vibrating blades and tailspins, are a good choice when fishing in deep water.

LEAD-HEAD BASS JIGS usually have a rubber skirt attached to the hook. Some bass jigs, however, feature hair or feathers. Many anglers tip jigs with live bait or they add some type of pork attractor to make a *jig-and-pig*. Perhaps the most popular attrac-

tor added to a rubber-skirted bass jig is the plastic crayfish. Called a *jig-and-craw* (above), these lures have won many national bass tournaments. Most bass jigs have nylon bristle weedguards. Jigs can be retrieved with a slow, steady up-and-down motion, bounced along bottom or jigged vertically.

JIGGING SPOONS are made of heavy metal. Most have a hammered, unpainted finish. They work well during coldwater periods when bass hold tight in timber or along cliff walls. Most spoons are heavy enough to be jigged vertically in water 50 feet deep.

VIBRATING BLADES are made of thin metal. Tie a snap to your line, then attach it to a hole in the lure's back. Jig these lures vertically or retrieve by reeling rapidly. Some anglers use them for trolling. The action is much like a vibrating crankbait.

TAILSPINS have a heavy lead body and a spinner on the tail. They work best for vertical jigging, but can be hopped along bottom or retrieved steadily.

Detecting strikes may be difficult because bass normally strike a jigging lure as it sinks. Keep the line tight to feel the light tap. Set the hook immediately.

Spoon Plugs

Spoon Plugs work best when trolled along a weedline. Use a stiff rod and a heavy-duty reel. If the plug is running properly, you can feel its vibrating action. Weeds will stop the action, but you can usually free the lure with a sharp yank. Use color-coded monofilament so you can return the lure to the same depth after you catch a fish. Troll Spoon Plugs at high speed and let them bump bottom. The large lip causes the lure to dive quickly, so you need only a short length of line. Choose the appropriate size Spoon Plug for the depth you're fishing. For example, use the Model 700 for depths of 15 to 20 feet; Model 100 for 12 to 15 feet; Model 200 for 9 to 12 feet; and Model 250 for 6 to 9 feet.

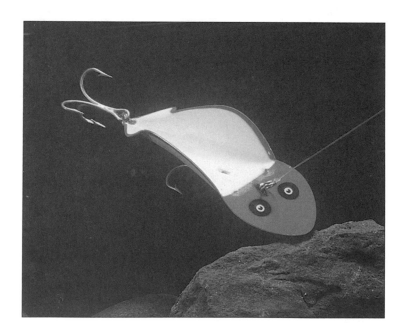

Straight-shaft Spinners

Straight-shaft spinners have one or more blades that rotate on a steel shaft. The single hook or treble may be hidden by a bucktail, rubber skirt or feathers. Spinners are usually not weedless, so you should retrieve them next to or just above cover. Many anglers tip spinners with live bait, pork rind or plastic attractors. Retrieve a straight-shaft spinner slowly and steadily. Some anglers prefer a reel-and-twitch retrieve. Spinners attract bass by their flash and vibration.

Weedless Spoons

Weedless spoons have been around a long time, but they're just as effective today as ever. Most have wire, plastic or bristle weedguards. They can be retrieved slowly through emergent weeds or other dense cover, crawled along bottom or skittered across the surface over thick weeds. Most anglers attach some type of rubber skirt or pork rind for extra action. The erratic, fluttering action is hard for bass to resist.

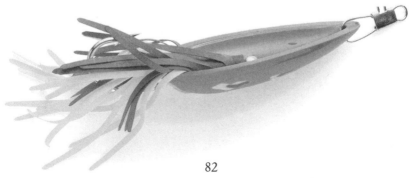

Fly Lures

Many fishermen overlook the fun and sport of fly fishing for bass. A 2-pound bass seems much larger when fought on a fly rod. Fly fishing is best in warm, calm weather when anglers work the surface of streams, ponds and weedy shallows of lakes. Most fly lures have bodies of cork, balsa or deer hair. Some are dressed with feathers or rubber skirts.

Bass bugs (right) need to be twitched on the surface to attract bass. After the cast, let the ripples settle and twitch the fly by either moving the rod tip or stripping in line. The fly should make a popping sound as it darts forward.

Experiment with retrieving subsurface flies (below); some days bass prefer a steady retrieve, on other days a stop-and-go retrieve works better.

Live Bait

The overwhelming majority of bass fishermen use artificial lures. But there is no doubt that live bait works better in many bass-fishing situations.

Trophy bass hunters swear by live bait. A glance at the record book shows that a 21-pound, 3-ounce largemouth was taken on a crayfish and a 20-pound, 15-ounce bass was caught on a nightcrawler.

Largemouths are more apt to strike live bait after a cold front, or when the water temperature is above or below their active feeding range. Sluggish bass grab only slow-moving food. But some artificial lures lose their action at slow speeds. Live bait, however, can be inched along bottom or dangled from a bobber. Lethargic bass take more time to examine their food, so they are more likely to spot an imitation.

Bass in extremely clear water can recognize a fake quickly. To catch these wary fish, some fishermen switch to live bait. They use the lightest line possible and keep their boats well away from the fishing zone to avoid spooking bass.

When fishing is slow, anglers often tip their lures with live bait such as worms or minnows. This adds scent appeal to the lure. A lively bait can also add action to a jig, spinner or spinnerbait, although it will ruin the action of a crankbait.

Largemouth bass eat a wider variety of natural foods than most gamefish. They will strike almost any live bait, from an inch-long grasshopper to a foot-long baitfish. The best baits have a lot of action and will stay lively despite repeated casting.

The type and size of bait must suit the fishing conditions. For example, some anglers use a technique called *freelining* to catch bass in thick weeds. They allow the bait to swim into dense cover. This method requires a large bait with enough power to pull the line through the tangle. Big

baits generally work best for big bass, especially when the fish are feeding actively. Smaller baits are better when bass are sluggish.

Nationwide, the most popular bass baits include waterdogs, frogs, crayfish and nightcrawlers.

Many experts consider the waterdog the number-one bait for largemouth bass. The waterdog is the immature stage, or *larva*, of the tiger salamander. Once the larval salamander turns into an adult, it is less appealing to bass.

Waterdogs can be purchased from bait shops or commercial growers in many areas of the country.

Some fishermen still rank frogs as the top bait for largemouth bass, but frog populations have plummeted as a result of disease and wetland drainage. Many anglers regard crayfish as the best bait for smallmouth bass, yet these crustaceans work equally well for largemouths. And while they rarely see earthworms, hungry bass will seldom ignore a gob of wiggling nightcrawlers.

Other live baits have gained popularity in certain regions. Bass in most estuaries prefer live shrimp to any other bait. In weedy lakes of Florida and Georgia, 8- to 12-inch golden shiners account for most trophy largemouths.

Fishermen along the Atlantic Coast are discovering that the American eel is a top bass producer. Known for their hardiness, eels will stay alive for days in a bucket of cool, damp grass.

The siren, a long, thin salamander found in south central and southeastern states, has an enticing, snake-like action. Other salamanders, called spring lizards, have been popular among generations of fishermen in the Southeast.

Hooking and Rigging Live Bait

Even the most irresistible live bait is worthless if not hooked and rigged properly. Choose the hook, sinker and line that best suits the conditions at hand.

When selecting a hook, consider the size of the bait and the type of cover. With a small hook and large bait, the bass is likely to steal your offering without getting hooked. If the hook is too large, the bait appears unnatural. Always use a weedless hook when fishing in heavy cover. Most have a springy wire weedguard that seats under the hook point.

Bait-saver tabs can be used to prevent your bait from wiggling off the hook. To make these tabs, punch out small circles of a plastic lid with a hole punch. Push on a tab, hook the bait through the lips, then add another tab.

The size and type of sinker depends on water depth, cover and bottom material. A 1/8- or 1/4-ounce sinker works well in water shallower than 15 feet, but deeper water requires more weight to keep the bait near bottom. A cone sinker is best for snaking baits through weeds and brush. A snag-resistant sinker such as a bottom-walker helps you to avoid constant hang-ups when fishing a rocky bottom.

When choosing line, keep in mind the water clarity, the potential for snagging, and the abrasiveness of the cover or bottom. Bass in clear water are most likely to strike live bait presented with clear, thin-diameter monofilament. Use heavier line in murky water or when snags are a problem. Hard-finish, abrasion-resistant line works best in tough weeds or in brush, timber or rocks.

Anglers should experiment to discover the rigging methods and fishing techniques that work best in their favorite bass waters. For example, minnows rigged on the back of a hair jig work great for casting weedlines or vertically jigging deep structure. Or minnows can be tipped on the back of a spinnerbait for covering lots of water on a weed flat. Finally, minnows are excellent when hooked through the lips and allowed to swim freely into a thick bank of shore-line weeds.

BASIC LIVE BAIT TECHNIQUES

•*Casting* enables you to drop live bait into a precise spot, such as a small pocket in the weeds, or the shade of a stump. It is the best technique for working a small area thoroughly.

•*Bobber-fishing* works best where casting or trolling would be impossible, such as in dense weeds. It is especially effective for sluggish bass in cold or warm water.

•*Trolling* allows you to cover a timberline, shoreline break or other long, straight edge quickly. Let out enough line so your sinker bounces along the bottom.

Selecting Lures & Bait

Many fishermen choose their lures by trial and error. They keep changing until they find one that catches bass. But choosing a lure is not a random choice for expert bass fishermen. They select a lure only after considering the following factors.

DEPTH. This is the prime concern in lure selection. For example, bass in deep water will seldom chase a lure retrieved just below the surface. Try to estimate the most probable depth based on the season, time of day, weather, water clarity and past experience on the body of water.

In water shallower than 10 feet, bass anglers use surface lures, spinnerbaits, spinners or shallow-running crankbaits. Lightly weighted plastic worms will also work. In deeper water, use deep-running or sinking crankbaits, jigging lures, heavily weighted plastic worms or spinnerbaits helicoptered to bottom. Live bait can be used in both shallow and deep water.

COVER. When fishing in thick weeds or brush, use a weedless spoon, Texas-rigged plastic worm, spinnerbait, brushguard jig, or any lure with a device to prevent snagging. When fishing with live bait, use a cone sinker and a weedless hook.

ACTIVITY LEVEL. The activity level of bass determines the size and action of the lure and the speed of the retrieve. Water temperature affects bass activity more than any other factor. However, weather conditions, especially cold fronts, can also play a role.

Bass in their optimum feeding range of 68° to 80°F are more likely to strike a larger, faster-moving lure or bait than bass in warmer or colder water. An 8-inch plastic worm may be a good choice at 75°F, but a 4-inch worm would probably work better at 83°F. In 55-degree water, bass will respond better to a smaller lure retrieved slowly. But lures like buzz baits would not work properly if retrieved slowly.

Live bait works well in cold water because it can be crawled along bottom or suspended from a bobber. Lures such as jigging spoons and small jigs are also good cold-water choices. Constantly lifting and dropping the lure through a tight school of bass will eventually pay off with a strike.

WATER CLARITY AND LIGHT LEVELS. Bass fishermen have different theories for selecting lure color. However, most agree that water clarity affects their choice of colors.

Many anglers insist that light-colored lures are better for fishing in clear water. But that does not explain the success of black or purple worms in clear waters. Fluorescent lures in yellow, chartreuse or orange seem to work best in murky water. Dark colors usually outproduce light colors on overcast days or at night.

When fishing at night or in a murky lake, use a noisy lure or bait. Good choices include a popper or chugger, a spinner bait with large blades, a buzz bait with a blade that ticks the shaft, or a crankbait with beads that rattle. Some anglers hook on a lively frog that will kick across the surface.

Beginning fishermen are often overwhelmed by the huge selection of bass lures at their local tackle shop. Many buy a large tackle box and fill each tray with a different lure. They never stick with one lure long enough to learn to use it properly.

Some beginners go to the opposite extreme. They catch a few fish on a particular lure, then refuse to change. The lure may work well at times, but too often it catches nothing.

Top bass fishermen contend that you cannot catch fish unless you have confidence in your *presentation*, meaning your choice of lure and how you retrieve it. When buying lures, select a few of each basic type, then learn how and when to use them. Catching fish is the quickest way to gain confidence in a lure.

The upcoming sections in this book explain how to choose the right lure for the right condition in a wide variety of lake types. But always keep one thing in mind: It doesn't matter what lure you have on or how you fish it if there aren't any bass in the area. Bass location is always the most important factor in the bass-catching equation.

4

HOW TO CATCH
BASS

Finding the Pattern

An observer at a professional bass tournament would hear a great deal of talk about finding the best *pattern*. When bass pros use this term, they are not referring to lure design. Instead, a pattern involves an elusive combination of two factors: bass location and the presentation needed to make fish bite. The pattern often changes from day to day and may even change several times a day.

The first step in unraveling a pattern is to locate the right type of fishing spot. Take into account the season, time of day and the weather. For example, on an overcast fall day, bass will most likely stay in the shallows. On a bright day in summer, bass may feed in open shallows in early morning. But as the sun moves higher, they will move deeper or into shaded areas of the shallows.

When scouting for bass, most anglers use some type of fast-moving lure like a crankbait or spinnerbait. Hungry bass will strike almost anything, so this technique is the quickest way to locate an active school. Rig several rods with different types of lures. This enables you to switch quickly without taking the time to tie on a new lure.

Concentrate on features within the most likely depth range, but occasionally move to shallower or deeper water. If you catch a bass, carefully note the exact depth and the type of cover and structure. Work the area thoroughly, but continue moving if you fail to catch another fish.

If you find an active school, try to avoid spooking the fish. Keep the boat at a distance and noise to a minimum.

Without changing lures, work the school until the bass quit biting. Use a landing net for only the largest fish. Grab smaller bass by the lower jaw. Untangling a lure from a net takes too much time.

Presentation becomes more important after you have skimmed the active fish from the school. Switching to a lure with a different action, color or size often triggers a strike immediately. Select a lure based on the situation and continue casting toward the fish. Experiment with various lures and retrieves to find the right combination.

Before you leave a good spot, note its exact location on your contour map. List any landmarks on shore that can be used as reference points for finding the area quickly in the future. Some fishermen toss out a marker, then return later to see if the fish have resumed feeding. When a spot no longer produces, try to duplicate the pattern by looking for a similar location nearby. If you found bass on a sharp-breaking point with bulrushes on top, chances are you will find bass on similar points elsewhere. If these areas fail to produce, the pattern has probably changed.

If the weather remains stable, the patterns you find one day will probably be repeated about the same time on the next day. But a change in weather will probably result in a new set of patterns.

In some instances, several patterns exist at the same time. Bass sometimes bite equally well in deep and shallow water, and the type of lure makes little difference. On these rare days, almost anyone can catch fish.

Finding a pattern for deepwater bass can be difficult and time-consuming. These fish often ignore fast-moving lures, so you may have to use a slower presentation. When you hook a fish in deep water, try to land it quickly. Otherwise, its frantic struggling may spook other bass in the school.

At times, there is no definite pattern. You may catch a bass here and there, but seldom more than one in any spot. Keep moving and cover as many areas as possible, including those places where you caught fish earlier in the day. Record trip results in a log book. A well-kept log can help you to find successful patterns when conditions are similar in future years.

Fishing for Bass on Structure

inding structure is the key to finding largemouth bass. Experts estimate that only 10 percent of a typical lake holds bass. And that 10 percent is usually around some type of structure. Fishermen who do not know how to find and fish structure have little chance for consistent success.

Structure simply means a change in the lake bottom. It could be a change in the depth or just a difference in the type of bottom material. Points, sunken islands, rock or gravel reefs, creek channels and shoreline breaks are typical structure in many waters.

Largemouths use structure as underwater highways. It provides easy access for bass moving from deep to shallow water. Structure also supplies bass with something to which they can relate. Given a choice, a bass will select a location near some type of recognizable feature.

The best bass structure has natural cover like weeds, flooded brush or timber, or man-made cover like riprap or brush shelters.

The quickest way to locate structure is to use an accurate contour map and a depth finder. With a little practice, you will learn to identify landmarks on shore for finding the general location of a good area. Then, by crisscrossing the

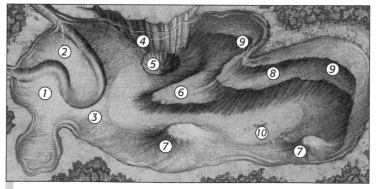

TYPICAL STRUCTURE includes: (1) shallow flat, (2) shallow ridge, or saddle, where a creek channel doubles back, (3) outside bend of a creek channel, (4) cliff wall, (5) deep hole, (6) extension of a point, (7) underwater hump, or sunken island, (8) breakline, (9) inside turn on a breakline, (10) rock reef.

area with your depth finder, you can pinpoint specific structure shown on the map. When you locate fish, note the exact depth. Chances are, bass on structure throughout the lake will be at the same depth.

Fishermen who spend a lot of time fishing one lake usually discover certain pieces of structure that routinely produce bass. In many cases, structure that seems identical produces nothing. Anglers have hired divers to inspect their secret spots, thinking there must be some difference that attracts bass. Often the diver finds nothing that could not be found in dozens of other areas. Bass sometimes choose spots for reasons we do not understand. The only solution for fishermen is to work many pieces of structure. Keep moving, try different depths and presentations until you find the right combination.

Where to Find Bass on Shallow Structure

Locating bass on shallow structure can be challenging even for the best anglers. Most lakes have an abundance of structure in shallow water, providing bass with an endless selection of feeding areas.

All types of structure can be found in either shallow or deep water. The term shallow structure refers to any structure in water 10 feet deep or less.

Begin your search for bass by working the most likely areas based on local reports, the season and your knowledge of the lake. Spend only a few minutes in each spot and keep moving until you find some active fish.

To reduce your scouting time, concentrate on a small section of the lake. Many anglers find it more productive to fish one creek arm thoroughly rather than spending the day roaming the lake.

In clear lakes, you can see shallow structure. Wear polarized glasses to find areas like the sharp break off the side of a weedy point, or a creek channel meandering through a flat. Bass in these areas can feed in shallow cover, then quickly retreat to deeper water. You may need a depth finder to spot structure in murky water.

When fishing on shallow structure, look for something slightly different from the surrounding area. Examples include a small section of reef that drops faster than the rest of the structure, a slight projection along the side of a point, or a shallow depression on top of a flat. These subtle variations frequently hold schools of bass.

SHALLOW STRUCTURE HOTSPOTS

•*Shallow flats* are prime feeding areas for largemouths. Flats are large expanses of water that have a uniform depth. Look for flats that border creek channels meandering through shallow reservoirs. Bass fishermen also work flats that rise gradually from bottom in mid-lake, or those that extend from shore.

•*Small creeks* provide bass with an easy-to-follow migration route leading from deep water into the shallows. They feed on the flats along both sides of the creek.

•*Flowing streams* wash bass foods into the back of a creek arm. Streams provide warmer water in spring and cooler water in summer.

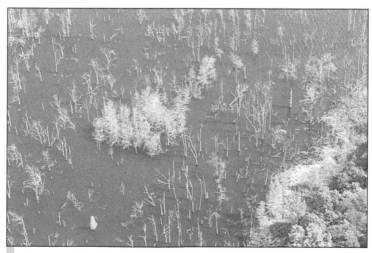

CLUMPS of timber or brush attract largemouths on flats. Look for bass in the thickest clumps or in those isolated from other cover.

99

•*Points* that taper gradually into deep water attract largemouths after spawning. Bass hang near these points for a few weeks before moving to deeper water.

•*Humps* are top bass producers in summer. Those near creek channels draw bass from deep water, especially if there is a ridge connecting the structures.

How to Catch Bass on Shallow Structure

Fishermen stand a much better chance of catching bass in shallow water than in deep water. Bass in the shallows are usually feeding and more likely to strike a lure.

But bass in the shallows pose two problems for anglers. The fish are often scattered. And they tend to spook easily, especially if the water is clear. To find bass on shallow

SHALLOW STRUCTURE often holds numbers of active largemouths. It's the perfect place to introduce young anglers to bass fishing.

structure, keep moving and use lures that can be cast and retrieved quickly so you can cover a lot of water. When you catch a fish, remember the exact location. You may want to return later for a few more casts.

When fishing in the shallows, avoid making unnecessary noises. Be especially careful not to drop anything on the bottom of the boat and do not run your outboard. Keep the boat as far away as possible and make long casts. If the water is very clear, watch the angle of the sun to avoid casting your shadow over the fish.

Almost any lure will work for fishing on shallow structure. The lure does not have to bump bottom to catch fish. A hungry bass in 6 feet of water will not hesitate to chase a buzz bait ripped across the surface, especially in warm water.

Most anglers prefer spinnerbaits or shallow-running crankbaits so they can cover a large area in a hurry. You may need a weedless lure if the structure has heavy weeds or brush. Carry a rod rigged with a plastic worm so you can work a brush clump or an isolated weedbed slowly and thoroughly. If a bass does take your lure in heavy cover, horse it back toward the boat to keep it from wrapping your line around weeds or limbs.

TECHNIQUES FOR FISHING ON SHALLOW STRUCTURE

•*Casting* is the best technique for working most types of shallow structure. Approach quietly and cut the outboard long before you reach the fishing area. Follow the edge of the structure while casting into the shallow water. Cover the shallows first, but if you do not catch fish, try deeper water along the structure's edge. On a gradually sloping shoreline you should angle some casts toward shore, others toward deeper water.

•*Fan-cast* from atop a shallow flat when the fish cannot be reached by casting from the edge. Quietly slip your boat onto the flat and tie on a spinnerbait or shallow-running crankbait. Use your trolling motor and move back and forth across the flat to cover it thoroughly.

•*Spot-cast* to any unusual cover on top of a flat, sunken island or point. A lone tree or bush, or an isolated clump of thick weeds is likely to hold bass. Cast a plastic worm or surface lure beyond the feature and retrieve the lure along the shaded side.

•*Position* your boat over the middle of the creek when fishing a narrow creek channel. Cast a crankbait to the shallows on either side of the channel, then retrieve the lure down the drop-off. Continue casting as you move down the channel.

•*Drifting* sometimes works well for fishing on shallow flats. Start at the upwind side, then let the wind push the boat slowly across the structure. Use your electric trolling motor to adjust the boat's direction. Always cast with the wind. This enables you to cover water the boat has not crossed. You can also cast farther with the wind at your back.

Where to Find Bass on Deep Structure

Before the advent of the depth finder, finding bass on deep structure was largely guesswork. Most fishermen worked shoreline structure because they could find it easily. Much of the deep, mid-lake structure was left unexplored.

The first anglers to buy depth finders enjoyed a fishing bonanza. Some schools of deepwater bass had never seen a lure. Fishing is not that easy today, but the angler who knows how to use a depth finder in conjunction with a lake map can consistently find bass on deep structure.

Prior to fishing any deep structure, explore the area thoroughly with your depth finder. Look for any variations on the structure, because these areas are most likely to hold bass. Make sure you understand the bottom configuration. This will make it easier to follow a contour and to keep your lure at a consistent depth.

When scouting a deep sunken island or flat, criss-cross the area several times. Toss a marker buoy onto the shallowest part of the sunken island or into the middle of the flat. The marker will serve as a reference point. Note the location of any projections or indentations along the edge of the structure, or any deep pockets on top.

To determine the shape of a submerged point, zigzag across it while edging farther into the lake. When you locate the tip of the point, throw out a marker. Then run the boat along each edge to find any irregularities.

Creek channels bordered by flooded timber are easy to follow. But channels without timber or brush can be difficult to trace. Watch your depth finder as you follow the edge. Drop enough markers to provide a picture of the channel configuration.

To find largemouths near a cliff wall, cruise slowly along the edge while watching the depth finder for signs of trees, brush or rock slides. Any type of projection different from the rest of the cliff will probably hold bass.

DEEP STRUCTURE HOTSPOTS

•*Berms*, or elevated banks, are formed by current depositing silt along the edges of a creek channel. Bass may hold

OUTSIDE BENDS (arrows) usually have the deepest water in a creek channel and, as a result, hold lots of bass. Steep walls or undercut banks were gouged out by current before the reservoir was formed.

103

on berms on both sides of a channel.

•*Roads* that once crossed creek channels may reveal the location of submerged bridge pilings. Bridge decks are usually removed before the reservoir is filled.

•*Points* that extend from shore to meet a creek channel provide ideal bass habitat. Largemouths that rest in the deep water of the creek channel must swim only a short distance to feed in heavy timber and brush on top of the point.

•*Intersections* of two creek channels concentrate largemouths, especially if there is ample flooded timber and brush bordering the creeks. If the junction has deep water, bass will generally stay in the area through winter.

•*Steep drop-offs* of deep points hold bass in summer, late fall and winter. Largemouths often hang near large boulders or piles of rocks.

•*Steep ledges* may provide the only bass cover in deep reservoirs. Scout for areas where wave action has eroded the rock, creating an overhang or causing the bank to cave in.

•*Rock reefs* 10 to 15 feet below the surface hold largemouth bass in summer, especially if surrounded by deep water. In clear lakes, bass may inhabit reefs 25 to 30 feet deep.

•*Shoreline breaks* provide the best structure in many bowl-shaped lakes. Bass congregate on inside turns and projections along a breakline. But largemouths may be anywhere on a break, especially where there is isolated cover or a distinct difference in the bottom material.

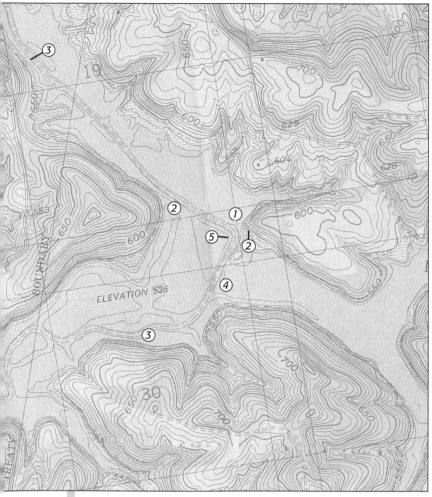

DEEP STRUCTURE in a reservoir includes: (1) outside bends of a creek channel, (2) points along a channel, (3) places where the channel runs next to shore, (4) intersections, (5) submerged point formed by a sharp bend.

How to Catch Bass on Deep Structure

Bass schooled in deep water are less likely to strike than fish in the shallows. But a lure retrieved slowly will usually tempt a few willing biters.

In warm water, you can generally locate bass along deep structure by using a fast presentation. Even though deep-water bass may not be feeding, chances are one or two fish out of the school will chase a fast-moving crankbait. Maneuver your boat along a drop-off as you cast toward shallow and deep water. When you catch a bass, stick with the crankbait and work the area until the fish quit biting. Then switch to a slower-moving lure and cover the area thoroughly. In cold water, fast-moving lures seldom catch bass. Use slower retrieves or try vertical jigging.

To fish irregular structure, such as a breakline with many sharp turns or the tip of a point, anchor your boat or hover above the spot. If you fish from a moving boat, it is difficult to keep your lure in the strike zone.

When fishing a long breakline with a few twists and turns, try speed trolling with deep-running crankbaits or Spoon Plugs. To find the proper depth, make several passes along the breakline while using lures that run at different depths. Note the exact location of any strike and continue to work the area until the fish stop biting. Then switch to a slower presentation, such as slow-hopping a plastic worm.

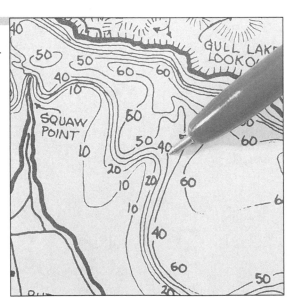

SUBMERGED POINTS are difficult to locate without a contour map and depth finder. Look for points projecting from a shoreline break or a sunken island.

TECHNIQUES FOR FISHING ON DEEP STRUCTURE

•*Cast* a sinking lure such as a plastic worm into the shallows along the outside bend of a creek channel. Bump it along bottom until it reaches the drop-off, then slow your retrieve as the lure drops down the slope.

•*Keep* the line tight as the lure sinks. Bass holding along the channel edge will grab a plastic worm or jigging lure as it drops. Set the hook immediately and pull the fish away from the cover as soon as possible.

•*Vertical jigging* is ideal for fishing along a steep ledge or any type of structure where bass school tightly. Drop a jigging spoon, tailspin or vibrating blade straight below the boat and jig it at different depths until you locate fish.

•*Parallel casting* works well for covering any sharp drop-off with a straight edge. Position the boat so you can cast a single-spin spinnerbait parallel to the ledge. Count the lure down to different depths to find bass.

•*Sharp-sloping points* are difficult to fish from deep water. As you retrieve a crankbait or single-spin spinnerbait, it loses contact with bottom. Position the boat in the shallows, cast into deep water and retrieve up the break.

•*Gradually-sloping points* should be fished by positioning the boat in deep water and making a long cast toward shore. Slowly retrieve a Carolina-rigged soft plastic lizard down the slope. Moving too close will spook fish in the shallows.

TIPS FOR FISHING ON DEEP STRUCTURE

•*Dip* your fishing rod into the water if you are having trouble getting a deep-running crankbait to the bottom. This makes the lure run 4 to 5 feet deeper. Use extra force to set the hook because of water resistance against the rod.

•*Reel* rapidly to make a deep-running crankbait dig into the bottom. The lip will kick up puffs of silt, much like a crayfish scurrying across bottom. This technique gives the plug an erratic action.

Fishing for Bass on Man-made Features

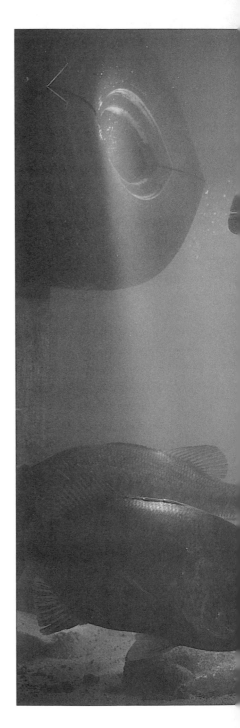

Nearly all bass waters show signs of human activity. Docks and boat houses surround the shoreline. In some lakes, tires, cement blocks and other debris litter the bottom. Some people consider these discarded items offensive, but you will not hear bass fishermen complaining. They know that many of these features provide excellent cover for bass.

Man-made features lie beneath the water in every reservoir. Occasionally, entire towns are flooded. Bass in reservoirs can be found near a wide array of features, from roadbeds and railroad tracks to the foundations of buildings.

In some waters, fisheries agencies or anglers place

fish attractors to provide habitat for bass. Attractors vary from clumps of brush or trees, to *stakebeds* with rows of upright slats on a wooden platform, to *crib shelters* made of large logs.

Bass will relate to man-made features in any lake, especially if they provide cover within the right depth range. But these features are more important in waters that lack adequate natural cover or structure. For example, in a murky lake with uniform depth and few weeds, bass scatter throughout the lake and become difficult to find. Man-made features in this type of lake will concentrate bass, making the fish easier to find and catch.

To find man-made features, obtain an up-to-date hydro-graphic map. Reservoir maps often show the location of features like submerged buildings, roadbeds and powerline crossings. Some maps also pinpoint the location of fish attractors. River charts show dredged channels, wingdams, levees and riprap shores.

Maps sometimes lack detail on man-made features, so fishermen must rely on local information and their depth finders. Liquid-crystal graphs and color videos can be especially valuable for reading man-made features. These units provide more detail than flashers, enabling you to distinguish between features like a man-made brush pile and a clump of weeds.

Where to Find Bass on Man-made Features

Bass prefer man-made features near some type of structure. Without deepwater refuge, the cover is of little value to bass. For example, you would be more likely to find bass near a bridge over a deep channel than a bridge over a shallow expanse of water.

Man-made features connected to a natural movement path will also concentrate bass. Earthen dams are often built across dry washes to create farm ponds. After the reservoir is filled, bass moving along the dry wash channel encounter the dam and gather along both sides.

Features near heavy natural cover will not hold as many bass as those that are isolated. Bass pay little attention to a brush pile placed in the middle of a thick weedbed. But the same brush pile would definitely hold bass if placed on a weedless hump.

Finding submerged features can be difficult. Fishermen sometimes mark their favorite spots with plastic jugs, while some conservation agencies pinpoint fish attractors with buoys. But most underwater features lack visible signs. To find them, you must have reliable information.

Local anglers or bait shop operators may be able to help you find man-made features. If not, keep an eye on other fishermen, especially those anchored in unusual locations. When they leave, check out the spot. You may find a school of bass hanging around a brush shelter or car body.

MAN-MADE HOTSPOTS

•*Shade* is the key to locating bass around man-made features. The fish often hold along the junction of shady and sunlit water. Note the angle of the sun and try to imagine where the shadow would fall under water.

•*Bridges* across narrow parts of a lake or reservoir funnel wind-blown foods into a small area. Look for bass hanging

RIPRAP prevents waves from eroding channel edges or steep shorelines. Look for bass where the bank drops quickly into deep water. Largemouths often hang near rocks close to shore.

tight to the pilings or near the concrete abutments next to shore.

•*Channels* dredged between two lakes or leading into a boat harbor may attract spawning largemouths. Watch for signs of nesting activity in the vegetation along both sides of the channel.

GOOD DOCKS provide ample shade. They have some weeds nearby, but not a dense stand that covers the area. Look for docks in water at least 3 feet deep and close to deeper water.

POOR DOCKS offer little shade. Some are in shallow areas with sparse weed growth. Largemouths use these docks only if they cannot find better cover elsewhere in the lake.

•*Junked vehicles* such as buses and cars or broken-down farm machinery provide homes for bass. Divers frequently observe bass inside old vehicles. Bass in pits and quarries gather around old mining equipment.

•*Crib shelters* are constructed from logs or railroad ties weighted down with large concrete blocks. Look for bass resting along the shaded side or hovering above these large attractors.

•*Brush piles* are made by sinking evergreen trees or bundles of large branches lashed together and weighted. They provide excellent cover for baitfish and aquatic insects, which in turn attract panfish and largemouths.

Where to Find Bass on Man-made Features in Reservoirs

Bass fishermen can easily find old buildings or any man-made feature that protrudes above the surface. But locating submerged features in a reservoir is difficult, even for the fisherman with an accurate hydrographic map.

If a good hydrographic map is not available, or if the map does not show man-made features, you still have other options.

You can wait for a *drawdown* to expose man-made features. Irrigation systems draw water from many reservoirs, gradually lowering the water level through summer and fall. Some reservoirs are drawn down rapidly in fall or winter to make room for heavy spring runoff. The water level may drop 40 feet below the normal summer stage. With the water this low, you can note the exact location of man-made features. Some fishermen take photographs of the lake bed during low water. When the basin fills, they know where to look for bass.

Maps made before the reservoir was filled can be helpful. U.S. Geological Survey maps, called *quad* maps, pinpoint the location of features such as houses, roads, railroad

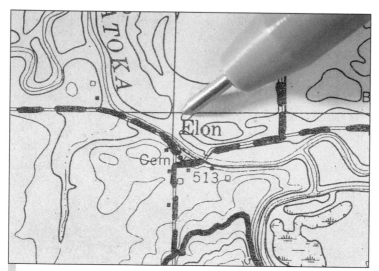

HOUSE FOUNDATIONS in flooded towns appear as solid black squares on a reservoir map. The dashed lines trace old roads. The solid line is the shoreline.

FENCE ROWS dividing open fields may provide the only cover in a large area. Look for bass near the largest trees or where fence rows cross.

116

tracks and ponds. Quad maps are available for almost all of the country. They also show land elevations, so if you know the surface elevation of the reservoir, you can easily calculate the depth of specific man-made features.

MAN-MADE HOTSPOTS IN RESERVOIRS

•*Powerline clearings* and boat roads were cut before the reservoir was flooded. Bass hold near the clearing rather than far back in the flooded timber.

•*Roadbeds,* especially those with hard surfaces, attract large-mouths. Work the ditches and any intersections with creek channels and other roads.

•*Railroad tracks* are usually built on elevated grades. Bass relate to the edge of the embankment just as they would to a natural breakline.

•*A cemetery* appears as a series of holes on a liquid-crystal graph. Before the reservoir is filled, the graves are excavated. Bass hang around the dirt piles.

How to Catch Bass on Man-made Features

Fishing along man-made features like riprap banks and roadbeds is little different than working natural features such as shoreline breaks and weedlines. Bass may scatter over a long distance, so you must keep moving until you find them.

But when fishing around man-made features like docks and bridge pilings, you know exactly where to look. To catch bass holding tight to these features, cast beyond the spot where the fish are likely to be. Then retrieve the lure so it passes only inches away. When fishing a straight-edged feature like a house foundation, chances are that bass will be lined up near the base of the wall along the shady side. Many fishermen make the mistake of casting at right angles to the wall, then pulling the lure away. With this technique, the lure is in the strike zone for only an instant, so it would take dozens of casts to cover the wall

117

completely. Instead, position your boat so you can cast parallel to the edge. Your lure will stay in the strike zone for most of the retrieve, enabling you to cover the edge quickly and thoroughly. This method also works well for fishing around natural structure and cover.

To work a specific spot like a bridge piling, jig vertically around the perimeter while working different depths. Some anglers intentionally mis-tune a crankbait so it veers toward hard-to-reach locations like the spaces between dock posts.

Flippin' works well for placing a lure in spots that are difficult to reach by casting. It may be hard to cast into the area between two docked boats or to drop a lure next to the inside wall of a duck blind. But you can flip a jig easily into either spot.

TECHNIQUES FOR FISHING ON MAN-MADE FEATURES

•*Cast* parallel to a riprap bank, then retrieve the lure along the slope at a consistent depth. Use a deep-diving crankbait or other lure that will skim the rocks. Move the boat in to fish shallower water; out for deeper water.

•*Look* for variations along a riprap bank such as branches, oversize rocks, points or bends. It pays to make a few casts into deep water, because bass may hang near rocks that have tumbled down the slope.

•*Cast* a crankbait or spinnerbait parallel to a channel wall. Retrieve the lure along bottom, keeping it as close to the wall as possible. Some anglers mis-tune a deep-running crankbait to make it slant toward the wall. Bend the eye in the direction you want the lure to run. The noise and erratic action of the lure bumping the wall often trigger strikes. Some fishermen walk along the wall, then vertically jig over the edge.

•*Toss* your lure into shade along a dock. Some fishermen prefer a 4- to 4½-foot casting rod to cast or skip the lure under the dock.

•*Retrieve* a Texas-rigged plastic worm or weedless jig-and-eel through a brush shelter. Slowly work the lure among the branches.

•*Cast* a deep-running or sinking crankbait parallel to a bridge pier. Some fishermen troll a figure-eight pattern around two adjacent bridge pilings. The lure will bump against each piling on the turns.

•*Lower* a jigging lure such as a tailspin or vibrating blade next to a bridge piling in deep water. Jig the lure vertically while you slowly work around the piling. Work different depths until you reach bottom.

•*Suspend* a waterdog or other lively bait to catch bass lurking inside a culvert. Lower the bait to the right depth on a jig head. Or use a split-shot or slip-bobber rig.

•*Flip* a lure into a duck blind with your boat near the entrance. Jig the lure around the inside edge of the blind. Then work the outer edge along the shady side.

Fishing for Bass in the Weeds

A largemouth tail-walking above the weeds as it tries to shake an artificial lure is a sight familiar to bass fishermen.

Weeds are the most common type of bass cover and certainly the most important. Bass fry crowd into dense weedbeds to hide from predators. Adult bass hide in weeds to ambush prey. The weeds provide homes for small insects which attract baitfish and other bass foods. Heavy mats of floating weeds prevent the sun's heat from penetrating the surface. Bass move into cool water below the

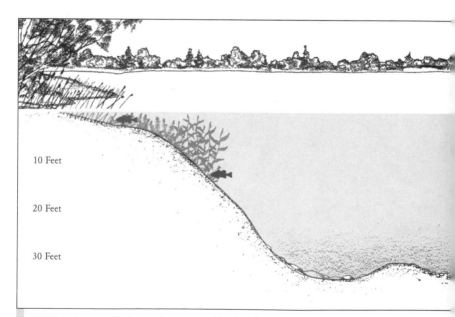

10 Feet

20 Feet

30 Feet

WEEDLINES usually form along drop-offs. This diagram shows submerged weeds that end abruptly at 15 feet. Weedlines also form where there is a distinct change in bottom type. Most bass hang near the edge of the weeds when the rest of the shallows becomes too warm.

Weeds perform yet another important function. Through the process of photosynthesis, they produce oxygen that is vital to the survival of fish.

The aquatic plants used by bass fall into the following categories:

SUBMERGED WEEDS. These weeds grow below the water, although some have flowers that extend above the surface. Water clarity determines how deep these plants will grow. In extremely clear water, they may get enough sunlight to flourish in depths of 30 feet or more. In murky lakes, they seldom grow in water deeper than 5 feet.

A distinct edge forms where the water becomes too deep for submerged weeds to grow. Called a weedline, this edge generally occurs at the same depth throughout a body of water. Weedlines are important bass-holding features.

FLOATING-LEAVED WEEDS. Some weeds, such as lily pads, have leaves that float on the surface. The broad leaves

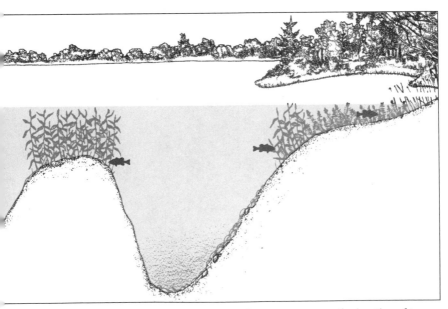

weedline, but some stay in shallow water or near the junction of two different weed types.

provide more shade than the leaves of most other plants. They offer excellent shallow-water cover for largemouths.

EMERGENT WEEDS. These plants protrude well above the surface. Often they form a band extending around much of a shoreline. Bass frequently spawn among emer-

gent weeds in 2 to 3 feet of water. Emergent weeds in deeper water may hold bass through the summer.

COMMON TYPES OF AQUATIC WEEDS

•*Water lilies* include some 15 species in North America. Round or heart-shaped leaves, called *pads*, float or stand slightly above the surface. The showy, cut-shaped flowers may be white, pink, blue or yellow, depending on the species. Lilies grow on muddy bottoms, usually in water shallower than 8 feet.

•*Water hyacinth* was introduced into the United States in the late 1800s. It is considered a nuisance in several southern states and California, where large beds float on the surface, covering entire lakes and waterways. It has rounded, shiny-green leaves and blue, white or violet flowers.

•*Bulrushes* include 55 types. Many grow in both fresh and brackish water. Most have round, leafless stems that taper to a slender point. Color varies from grayish green to dark green. Small brownish flowers appear at the top of the stem. These rooted plants may grow to 5 feet above the surface.

•*Cattails* are named for the brownish, fur-like flower at the tip of the stem. All four species prefer soft bottoms and can live in fresh or brackish water. The leaves are long and flat, varying from yellowish green to dark green. They sprout from large roots, or *rhizomes*. Cattails can grow as high as 8 feet above the water.

•*Pondweeds* total over 50 species. These rooted plants grow in fresh or brackish water. Leaves may be thread-like or broad; broad-leaved types are called *cabbage*. Most species have submerged leaves, but some have floating leaves. Most pondweeds have flowering heads, or *spikes*, that protrude above the surface.

•*Coontail* forms dense blankets as much as 10 feet thick. A stand is made up of plants anchored on the soft bottom along with pieces of coontail that have broken off, but continue to live. Each branch, with its thick cluster of narrow leaves, resembles a raccoon's tail. Color varies from olive to dark green among the six kinds.

•*Milfoil* includes 13 types, some of which grow in brackish water. Sometimes confused with coontail, milfoil often has pinkish or reddish, rather than greenish stems. It grows on soft bottoms and may form a dense layer up to 10 feet thick. Eurasian water milfoil (p. 131), though an unwelcome invader in much of the country, makes excellent bass cover.

•*Hydrilla,* a fast-spreading exotic, was first discovered in Florida and has spread through much of the South. It requires little sunlight, so it grows to greater depths and in darker waters than most other aquatic plants. Although it causes serious navigation problems in shallow lakes, it has revitalized the fisheries in many old reservoirs.

Where and How to Catch Bass in Shallow Weeds

Bass fishermen in natural lakes catch more largemouths in shallow weeds than in any other type of cover. Shallow weeds include any type of emergent, floating-leaved or submerged plant in water 10 feet or less. The type of weed matters little to bass, as long as it provides adequate cover.

The best times to find bass in shallow vegetation are spring and early fall. In summer, weeds serve mainly as morning and evening feeding grounds. But some bass stay in the weeds all summer if the cover is dense enough to block out sunlight.

Shallow weeds near deep water usually hold the most bass. Given a choice, bass will choose a weedbed near a drop-off over one located in the middle of a large, shallow area. Avoid weedbeds so thick that bass would have difficulty moving about.

SHALLOW WEED HOTSPOTS

•*Pockets in floating-leaved weeds* such as lily pads serve as ambush points for feeding largemouths. Avoid large stands of pads in very shallow water with no deeper water nearby.

•*Edges of emergent weeds* such as bulrushes are top shallow-water locations. The inside edge of a weedbed may hold as many as the outside edge. Look for bass in any boat lanes or openings in the weeds.

•*Clumps of emergent weeds* often break away from dense mats along shore. These clumps float about the lake, providing temporary cover for largemouth bass, usually in early spring.

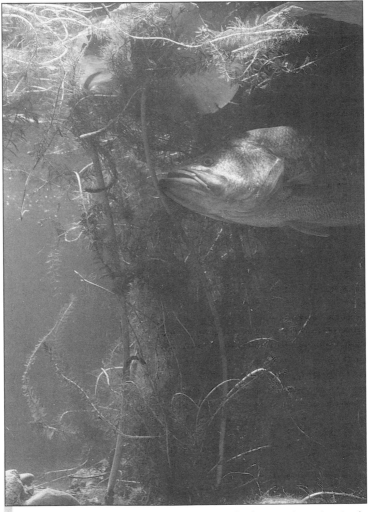

SLOP consists of various floating-leaved and submerged weeds mixed with filamentous, or moss-like algae. The water temperature may be 10 degrees cooler below the slop.

Fishing in shallow weeds requires special equipment. Most anglers prefer a powerful rod and a high-speed, baitcasting reel. Once you hook a bass, pull as hard as your equipment allows to head the bass toward the surface. Hold the rod tip high as you reel. Exert strong pressure to keep its head up. If you allow the bass to dive into dense cover, it will probably tangle your line around the stems and break free. Strong pressure also reduces the chance of the bass throwing the hook when it jumps.

Abrasion-resistant monofilament, generally 12- to 17-pound test, works well for most weed-fishing situations. Some fishermen use mono up to 30-pound test when fishing in dense weedbeds. Heavy line does not seem to spook bass in thick cover.

Weedless lures are a must for fishing in most shallow weeds. You may be able to snake a standard lure through scattered weeds, but even moderately dense weeds will foul your hooks and ruin the lure's action. Manufacturers make various types of weedguards out of wire, plastic, nylon bristle and stiff monofilament. However, if the weedguard is too stiff, it reduces your chances of hooking bass.

Although they lack weedless hooks, Texas-rigged plastic worms and spinnerbaits are among the most weed-resistant lures. Some fishermen bend their hook points slightly toward the hook shank. The point is less likely to pick up weeds, but is exposed enough to hook a bass.

Angling in shallow weeds demands accurate casting. Bass in dense weeds may be reluctant to chase a lure. You must be able to hit small pockets or to cast parallel to a weed edge.

Fly casting is an extremely effective method of presenting a lure into a small opening in shallow weeds. But horsing a big bass out of heavy cover will test the tackle of any fly fisherman.

Many bass fishermen swear by live bait rigged on a weedless hook. You can dap a frog, salamander or minnow into holes in the weeds; you can let the bait swim through cover with a free line; or you can suspend it from a bobber. Some anglers gently lob the bait a short distance, then skitter it across weedtops. Long casts will kill most live baits quickly.

TECHNIQUES FOR FISHING IN SHALLOW WEEDS

•*Spot-cast* into pockets. Let a sinking lure like a bass jig or weedless spoon flutter downward into the opening. If using a topwater lure, let it rest briefly before twitching it.

•*Cast* parallel to weed edges. Drop a spinnerbait, buzz bait or topwater lure within a few inches of the weeds, then retrieve it as close as possible to the margin.

•*Skitter* a weedless spoon over slop or floating-leaved weeds. Hold the rod tip high and reel rapidly to keep the lure on the surface.

127

•*Flip* into tight spots by pulling off about two rod-lengths of line. Let half of the line dangle from the rod tip; hold the other half in your free hand. Keeping the tip up, point the rod in the direction of the target. Swing the lure toward your body. Flip the lure with a short, upward snap of the rod tip. At the same time, release the line in your free hand. If the water is deep, allow the line to flow from the spool as the lure sinks.

•*Twitch* a fly rod popper in an open pocket, then let it lie motionless until the ripples subside. Set the hook at the slightest disturbance. Hold the rod tip high to keep the fish's head above the weeds. If the bass dives, it will probably become entangled in the thick vegetation.

•*Hook* an 8- to 12-inch golden shiner through the tail for freelining in dense vegetation like hyacinth beds. Use a 3/0 to 6/0 hook. If casting and retrieving, hook the shiner through the lips. Open your bail or put the reel in free-spool, then let the shiner swim through the weedy tangle. Some bass fishermen rig shiners with a bobber and work the baitfish along the edges of large weedbeds.

TIPS FOR FISHING IN SHALLOW WEEDS

•*Wear* polarized glasses to cut glare while scouting variations in the weeds. Avoid unnecessary noise that might spook the fish.

•*Cut* the leading hook from each of the trebles to make a surface lure more weedless. Some anglers replace the hooks with weedguard trebles.

•*Sharpen* the edges of the prop on your trolling motor, using a file. The sharp edges cut weed stems so they don't foul the prop.

Where and How to Catch Bass in Deep Weeds

The secret to catching bass in deep weeds is to find a weedline. You can catch some largemouths in a wide expanse

TALL WEEDS provide bass with shade. Some types of pondweeds may grow to the surface in water as deep as 15 feet.

of deep weeds, but to improve your odds, concentrate on the edges.

Weedlines concentrate largemouths. When feeding, bass cruise along the edge or leave the weedline to move into shallow water. To rest, they sometimes retreat a short distance into the weeds.

Variations along the weedline hold the most fish. Bass recognize and use these specific spots as resting sites or ambush points. Look for a pocket or even a slight indentation along the edge. Largemouths also school around points of weeds that project farther out than the rest of the weedline.

Deep, weedy flats in clear lakes hold some bass, especially in summer. The fish hang just above the weeds while cruising the flat. Finding the bass may be difficult because they can be anywhere on the flat.

In a clear lake, weeds may grow to depths of 20 or 25 feet. But with a depth finder and a little practice, locating a deep weedline is not as difficult as you might expect. When you find a weedline, throw out one or more markers along the edge, keeping them just inside the weeds.

Use your trolling motor or drift along the weedline while casting a crankbait. Or troll a deep-running crankbait or Spoon Plug along the edge. Stay just outside the markers while letting out enough line so the lure ticks bottom. Some fishermen use metered monofilament so they can easily find the same depth after catching a bass.

If you catch a bass while trolling or drifting, it is probably an active fish within a school. Mark the spot, then work it thoroughly. You may have to switch to a slower presentation to catch more fish.

If you do not have a depth finder, you must rely on your sense of feel. When your lure tracks through weeds, it catches momentarily, pulls loose, then catches again. Veer toward deeper water until you no longer feel weeds, then slowly angle back toward the weedline.

Most lure types used in shallow weeds will also work in deep weeds. But you may need a larger sinker with your plastic worm, a heavier spinnerbait or jig, or a deeper-diving crankbait.

IN MANY LAKES AND RESERVOIRS of North America, Eurasian water milfoil has gained a strong foothold. In the eyes of many recreational boaters, this weed is the most troublesome of all aquatic plants. While native milfoil species seldom grow in water deeper than 10 feet, Eurasian milfoil thrives in water as deep as 30, so it covers a much greater portion of a lake bed. Shortly after it gets into a lake, it overwhelms other native aquatic plants and often crowds them out completely.

Some anglers, however, are pleased with the spread of this weed because many milfoil-infested lakes are producing more and bigger largemouths than ever before.

Eurasian milfoil is easily confused with several native North American milfoil species. But it can usually be distinguished by its finer, more closely spaced leaflets.

Eurasion Milfoil

Eurasian water milfoil sprig

Eurasian milfoil leaflet

Northern milfoil leaflet

Bass along a deep weedline sometimes ignore artificial lures. If the fish are not feeding, live bait may be the only solution. Using a slip-sinker rig, cast parallel to the weedline, then inch the bait toward the boat. Or suspend the bait from a slip-bobber. Retrieve it slowly or let the wind push it along the edge of the weeds.

TECHNIQUES FOR FISHING IN DEEP WEEDS

•*Locate* a deep weedline with a flasher or graph. While over the weeds, you'll see a wide band of blips or marks above the bottom. The marks will disappear when you cross the weedline.

•*Rip* a crankbait through brittle weeds, such as cabbage, by reeling rapidly. Use a stiff rod so you can jerk the lure free from weeds. The lure will dart erratically when it breaks loose, often coaxing a strike.

•*Work* the weedline by casting a deep-running crankbait, plastic worm or jig-and-pig and retrieving it parallel to the weedline. Cast a shallower-running crankbait to the top of the drop-off and retrieve it down the slope just above the weedtops. Or toss a spinnerbait into the shallows and reel it toward the drop-off.

•*Yo-yo* a 3/4- to 1-ounce brushguard jig with a pork or soft-plastic trailer in dense weedbeds. Make a short cast, shake your rod tip to get the lure down through the weeds, yo-yo it a few times, then reel up and cast again.

Fishing for Bass in Flooded Timber & Brush

When a bass feels the sting of a hook, its first reaction is to head for cover. And if that cover happens to be nearby trees or brush, the ensuing battle will test the skill of any angler.

Although it may be difficult to fight and land a bass in woody cover, fishermen who know how to work timber and brush rarely fail to catch bass.

Dams on large rivers have flooded vast expanses of timber and brush over the past few decades. After a reservoir fills, over 100 feet of water may cover the trees. In some impoundments, the entire basin is flooded timber with the exception of farm fields, roads and towns.

A low dam on a river will not cover an entire forest, but it will flood timber and brush in the backwaters. These trees also rot off in time. Waves pounding on stumps in shallow water wash soil away from the bases, exposing the root systems. The spaces between the roots make ideal bass cover. Stumps in shallow areas of reservoirs also have exposed roots under water.

Submerged trees may last indefinitely. Timber that protrudes above water eventually rots off at the water line, leaving only partially exposed trunks.

In some cases, the U.S. Army Corps of Engineers or other government agencies cuts the trees as a reservoir is filling. Once filled, the reservoir appears to be void of timber, but it has a forest of tree trunks several feet below the surface. Occasionally, loggers *clearcut* most of the trees before a

reservoir is created, leaving only stumps. Although tall timber may be hard to find, the chances of it holding bass are better than if the reservoir was filled with trees.

Some reservoir maps show the location of timber; some do not. If your map lacks such information, obtain a quad map, which shows the location of woodlands before the reservoir was filled. Chances are, the trees will still be there.

Flooded brush decays much faster than timber. You may find brush in deep water in some new reservoirs, but in older ones, brush grows mainly in the shallows. During prolonged periods of low water, brush flourishes along shore. When the water level returns to normal, the brush is submerged, providing excellent bass habitat.

Bass in natural lakes and river backwaters seek cover in flooded brush, especially during spring and early summer when runoff raises water levels. The brush harbors foods such as minnows and insects.

Anglers who spend a lot of time fishing around timber know that certain types of trees are better than others. Generally, the largest trees or those with the most branches attract the most fish. Cedar trees, for example, with their dense network of branches, are consistent bass producers.

In southern lakes and sloughs, water-dwelling trees such as cypress provide homes for largemouths. Erosion along riverbanks often results in trees tumbling into the water. The branches offer cover and break the current.

In steep-walled reservoirs, rock slides carry trees and brush down the slope and into the water. The trees may provide the only cover along a cliff wall. In lakes and ponds that lack good shoreline cover, fishermen sometimes fell trees into the water, then cable the tree to the stump.

Where and How to Catch Bass in Shallow Timber and Brush

When searching for feeding bass in a reservoir, most anglers head for a patch of shallow timber or brush.

Bass use shallow timber and brush the same way they use shallow weeds. It offers a protected spawning area in spring, a morning and evening feeding zone in summer and an all-day feeding area in early fall. Bass abandon this cover in late fall and winter.

The best shallow timber and brush is generally near deep water. Look for bass around isolated patches, along a distinct tree line or brushline, and in deep pockets on brush-

or timber-covered flats. Fishermen can sometimes see clues that reveal the location of submerged timber and brush. A small limb extending above the surface may be part of a large tree. *Stickups*, or the tips of small branches, pinpoint the location of submerged brush. A tilted log in open water probably means a tree has floated in and lodged along a drop-off. A clump of trees or brush standing higher than others nearby indicates an underwater hump.

SHALLOW TIMBER AND BRUSH HOTSPOTS

•*Isolated patches of trees* or brush concentrate bass. A small stand of trees away from other cover is more likely to hold

DOWNED TREES offer several types of cover for bass. The fish hang among the branches or under the main trunk. If the entire tree has toppled into the water, look for bass among the roots.

TREE LINES and brushlines are similar to weedlines. Look for bass along the edge or several feet inside the cover. Sharp bends, pockets or points along the edge hold more bass than straight portions.

bass than a similar stand within a flooded forest or near a large weedbed.

•*Brushy flats near deep water* often hold feeding bass. If the flat is bordered by a distinct line of brush, fish mainly along the edge. Bass also hold in the thickest clumps of brush on the flat.

Weedless lures are a must for fishing in brush and stumps. Spinnerbaits and Texas-rigged plastic worms were developed specifically for this purpose. Other popular lures include buzz baits or weedless spoons and brushguard jigs tipped with pork attractors.

With a little practice, you can learn how to work a crankbait through openings in the brush and how to bounce it off stumps without snagging.

Casting accuracy is important when fishing in shallow timber and brush. A bass holding tight under a log may refuse a lure that passes more than a foot or two away. But when bass begin to feed, they move out of their hiding spots to cruise about in openings between the trees or brush. Anglers often ignore these open areas, thinking that all bass are near cover. Largemouths in clear water generally hold tighter to cover than bass in murky water.

Use heavy, abrasion-resistant line for fishing in timber or brush. The constant friction of line against limbs will soon cause fraying. Check your line frequently. Tug on your knots after catching a bass. A rough spot on the line or a weak knot could result in a lost trophy. Cut off a few feet of line and retie your knots several times a day.

TECHNIQUES FOR FISHING IN SHALLOW TIMBER AND BRUSH

•*Cast* a spinnerbait several feet beyond a tree or stump. Angle your cast so you can bring the lure within a few inches of the object. Buzz the lure across the surface by holding the rod tip high and reeling rapidly. Stop reeling when the lure is next to the tree. Helicopter the spinnerbait down along the tree by dropping your rod tip quickly. Follow the lure with your rod tip, keeping the line tight as the lure sinks. Watch your line carefully. Set the hook the instant you see the line twitch or feel a light tap. Bass usually strike as the lure sinks or just after you begin the retrieve.

•*Flip* a jig-and-pig, jig-and-craw or plastic worm into openings between stumps, trees or brush. Drop the lure into areas with the heaviest shade. Wait until the lure hits bottom. Hop the jig through the opening by lifting the rod tip, then lowering the rod to ease the lure back to bottom.

BUMP a crankbait against the side of a log or bush. The erratic action may tempt a bass. A big-lipped crankbait will bounce off branches, reducing snags.

•*Float* an unweighted plastic lizard or worm over shallow brush. Twitch the lure as you retrieve it slowly. Watch for a slurp that signals a strike.

Where and How to Catch Bass in Deep Timber and Brush

If you ran a liquid-crystal graph over a submerged forest, you would probably see a large number of fish scattered among the trees. And a good share of them would be bass.

A graph is valuable for locating bass in deep timber because it enables you to distinguish fish from tree limbs. On a flasher, bass look much like the branches.

Finding bass in deep timber and brush may be difficult, especially in a reservoir that has a lot of trees. The secret is to locate edges or isolated clumps of woody cover.

Prime locations include tree lines along structure such as creek channels. Other good locations include farm fields, orchards, windbreaks or shelterbelts, and powerline clearings. Look for bass in brushlines along road ditches and fencelines. They also congregate in timber and brush on sunken islands, points and deep flats.

In clear-cut areas, stumps may provide the only bass cover. If your depth finder shows a jagged bottom, you may be over a submerged stump field.

In summer, look for bass in timber or brush from 15 to 25 feet deep. Fish brushlines or timberlines much as you would a weedline. Use a deep-running crankbait to find the bass. Then switch to a plastic worm or a brushguard jig. Vary the depth of your retrieve because bass may be suspended halfway up the trees.

During late fall and winter, many bass are caught by vertical jigging in 30 to 40 feet of water. Start jigging at 10 to 15 feet and work your way down. After a few warm days in winter, bass often gather near the surface. Catch them by retrieving a surface lure just above the treetops.

Some anglers prefer 20- to 30-pound test braided Dacron line or the new "super lines" for fishing in deep timber and brush. These lines have almost no stretch, so they signal a bite better than mono. They also resist nicks and abrasions better than monofilament.

TECHNIQUES FOR FISHING IN DEEP TIMBER AND BRUSH

•*Cast* a plastic worm, jig-and-craw or jig-and-pig past the timber and let the lure fall as far as possible into the branches. Slowly work the lure through the limbs watching your line for a twitch. Make several casts into a single tree to ensure that you've covered the timber thoroughly.

•*Position* your boat as close as possible to a large tree. Drop a jig-and-pig, tailspin, jigging spoon or a jig tipped with a plastic grub down through the limbs, keeping it close to the trunk. Twitch the jig, then keep a tight line as it sinks. This lets you detect even the lightest tap. Jig around the tree at different depths.

HOW TO FISH A PLASTIC WORM IN DEEP TIMBER AND BRUSH

EASE a Texas-rigged plastic worm over the branches. The worm will occasionally catch on limbs or twigs as you retrieve.

Drop the rod tip to give a few inches of slack, then twitch it gently to flip the worm over the branch. Keep the rod tip up after the sinker comes free.

WATCH your line as the worm settles. A strike may feel like a sharp tap or your line may move off to the side. Set the hook immediately.

TIPS FOR FISHING IN DEEP TIMBER AND BRUSH

•*Peg* a cone sinker when using a Texas-rigged plastic worm in brush or timber. Wedge a toothpick into the sinker, then cut off the excess with a nail clipper. Pegging the sinker prevents it from sliding away from the worm when it catches on a branch.

•*Free* a snagged lure with a plug-knocker. Attach wire pigtails to a heavy weight such as an 8- to 12-ounce sinker. Tie a heavy cord to the weight, then slip the fishing line into the pigtails. Holding on to the cord, slide the weight down the line to knock the plug loose.

5

SPECIAL
SITUATIONS

For consistent bass-fishing success, you should know how to deal with special situations. Included in this chapter are some of the toughest fishing problems, along with some opportunities that many bass fishermen ignore.

Tough fishing conditions are not unusual. They begin in spring when bass complete spawning and the females refuse to bite. Heavy spring rains cause drastic fluctuations in water levels and clarity, both of which can slow fishing. In late spring and summer, cold fronts often pass through only a few days apart, bringing fishing to a standstill. By mid-summer, abundant food makes bass less inclined to bite. In late fall and winter, bass spend much of their time suspended in deep water where catching them can be difficult.

The difference between a good bass fisherman and an expert is the ability to solve these tough fishing problems. For example, when reservoirs become muddy after a heavy rainfall, most anglers give up. But the expert fisherman finds a creek arm with a clear stream flowing in and enjoys some of the best fishing of the year.

Successful anglers have another important skill: They know how to recognize and take advantage of fishing opportunities. Rivers and streams, for example, can provide quality angling in summer when fishing on lakes and reservoirs is slow. And fishermen who master night-fishing techniques often catch bass when daytime anglers fail.

Sometimes these opportunities last only a moment. An inexperienced fisherman will motor past a flock of diving gulls, paying little attention to the noisy birds. But the expert knows that gulls wheeling over the water often reveal a school of largemouths feeding on shad near the surface. He races to the spot and boats several bass before the school disappears.

Cold Fronts

Few anglers agree as to why bass fishing slows down after a cold front. But all agree that it does slow down. And if the cold front is severe, bass may not bite for several days.

Some fishermen blame the poor fishing on a rising barometer. But studies have failed to confirm that barometric

pressure alone has any effect on fishing. Falling water temperature may have some impact. Even though the air temperature may change drastically, the water temperature changes little.

The most logical explanation is that extremely clear skies following a cold front allow more sunlight to reach the water. The strong light drives bass into deeper water or heavier cover. Divers have reported seeing bass buried in deep weeds with only their tails sticking out. The fish generally remain inactive for 1 to 2 days after the front passes. If bass do not have access to deep water, they bury in the thickest weeds in the shallows. If possible, you should avoid fishing in shallow bays following a cold front. These areas cool faster than the rest of the lake, making the effects of the front more noticeable to bass. Rivers and other murky waters continue to produce bass after a cold front. The turbid water allows little light penetration, despite the clear skies.

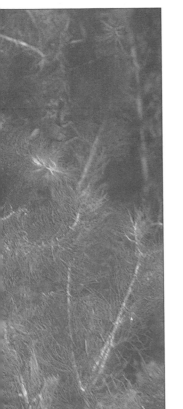

Catching bass holding tight to thick cover requires pinpoint casting. Most fishermen use small lures, slow retrieves and light lines to tempt lethargic bass.

Flippin' or simply dapping into heavy cover enables you to present a lure within a few inches of a bass. Jig the lure slowly, but pause occasionally so it hangs motionless. Sometimes a bass will stare at a lure several minutes before striking. Live bait such as a nightcrawler may be the best solution for catching largemouths after a cold front. Bass examine their food closely, often ignoring everything but the real thing.

If a bass does bite, it often takes only a halfhearted nip at the lure or bait. Keep a tight line and watch carefully for the slightest twitch.

Suspended Bass

Finding suspended bass is easy; catching them is another matter. Fishermen scouting open water with depth finders sometimes spot bass far above bottom. But if the fish are in open water deeper than 20 feet, angling for them is probably a waste of time because they are not actively feeding.

Bass suspended near some type of cover are easier to catch. Fishermen on reservoirs often catch suspended bass by vertically jigging along sheer cliffs or in flooded timber at depths up to 50 feet. Begin by dropping a jigging spoon, vibrating blade or tailspin close to standing timber. Jig vertically, working the upper branches first. Gradually lower the lure, stopping to jig every few feet. Continue jigging all the way to bottom.

Bass often suspend below large schools of panfish in open water. The small fish usually hang from 5 to 10 feet below the surface with the bass several feet below them. On calm mornings and evenings, the panfish dimple the surface while feeding on tiny insects. Many anglers have seen the quiet water disturbed by the occasional swirls of bass grabbing small panfish. If you see this happening, try drawing bass to the surface with a topwater lure. Slowly walk the lure across the surface, creating a disturbance to attract suspended bass. Keep moving and cover as much water as possible. Some anglers use the countdown method if bass refuse surface lures. Cast into the vicinity of the bass, then count as the lure sinks. Begin your retrieve at different counts until you catch a bass. Then count the lure down to the same depth on succeeding casts.

Another effective technique for catching suspended bass is dangling live bait from a slip-bobber. As the bait sinks, the line slips through the bobber and stops at a sliding knot positioned at the desired depth. Adjust the knot so the bait hangs just above the fish.

Largemouths suspended in open water are more likely to strike if you use light line. A line weight of 6 to 8 pounds will subdue even the largest bass in water free of obstructions.

Hot Weather

Most people begin their summer vacations about the time bass fishing takes its hot-weather nosedive. Even the best fishermen sometimes have trouble catching bass in midsummer.

There are many reasons for poor bass fishing during hot weather. Most significant is the abundant food supply. Baitfish hatched in spring reach a size attractive to bass in midsummer. Sunfish and perch, for example, have reached 1 to 2 inches, a size large enough to tempt bass. Largemouths pick off the young baitfish while cruising the edges of weedbeds. With natural food so easy to find, artificial lures have less appeal.

Midsummer finds sunlight penetration at its highest. With the sun directly overhead, bass must move deeper or find shade. Bridges, docks and other solid overhead cover may provide enough shade to keep the surface water several degrees cooler than the surrounding area. Slop or other matted vegetation may offer the only shade in shallow lakes that lack man-made cover such as docks. If the water temperature exceeds 80°F, bass look for cooler water in the depths, around springs or near coldwater tributaries. If they cannot find water cooler than 80°F, they become sluggish and eat very little.

Many anglers assume that largemouths do not feed during midsummer. But with the exception of shallow lakes in the Deep South, bass eat more in midsummer than at any other time of the year. In one study of a northern lake, bass ate 222 percent more food per day during July and August than they ate in May and June.

These figures prove you can catch bass in summer. But you must be in the right place at the right time. When food is plentiful, it takes only a few minutes for a bass to eat its fill for the day.

If the weather is hot, clear and calm, these short feeding bursts take place at dusk, dawn or at night. Bass feed on the same shallow flats used at other times of the year. But you can also find active schools in deep water. If you catch bass at a certain time one day, they will probably feed about the same time the next day, unless the weather changes. Bass sometimes bite throughout the day if the weather if overcast, rainy or windy. The low-light conditions and slightly cooler surface temperature cause bass to leave thick cover or to move shallower to feed.

Unless the water temperature exceeds 80°F, hot-weather fishing requires no special techniques. Use presentations appropriate for the situation.

At temperatures above 80°F, small lures and slow retrieves work best. When fishing in slop, slowly reel a surface lure over the matted weeds. Or flip a 4-inch plastic worm into openings in the weeds. In deep water, try vertically jigging with a spoon, tailspin or jig-and-eel. If bass refuse these offerings, live bait may be the answer.

Clear Water

Ultraclear water presents one of bass fishing's toughest challenges. In some canyon reservoirs, strip pits and natural lakes, fishermen have observed bass cruising in water 20 feet deep. And when you can see the bass, the bass can see you.

Finding bass in clear water may be more difficult than finding them in murky water because the fish may go very deep to escape sunlight and warm temperatures. In canyon reservoirs, bass have been found at depths exceeding 100 feet. In murky lakes with heavy algae blooms, bass are confined to the shallows because the depths lack oxygen.

Not all bass go deep on sunny days. If there is brush and floating, matted weeds in the shallows, they may simply move into the shade. Overhanging cliffs, docks, bridges and other overhead cover also offer ample shade. These shallow-water fish are not easy to catch, however. They hold extremely close to the available cover so you must be extremely accurate with your casts. Under this type of cover, bass will remain in the shallows all day.

When fishing in clear, shallow water, wear neutral-colored clothing, keep a low profile and avoid moving suddenly or casting your shadow over the fish. Although bass in shallow water tend to be spooky, they are still easier to catch than largemouths in deep water.

Largemouths in clear lakes bite best at dusk or dawn, and on windy or overcast days when light penetration is at a minimum. Fishermen on some crystal-clear lakes catch the majority of their bass at night, especially in summer. After the sun goes down bass in the depths move into shallower water, while bass in shallow water move out of heavy cover and cruise the weed edges looking for an easy meal.

Fast retrieves work best in clear water. A slow retrieve gives bass too much time to inspect your lure. Long casts help you avoid spooking the fish. To increase your casting distance, use spinning tackle with 4- to 10-pound monofilament. Avoid high-visibility line. Also avoid fluorescent or gaudy lures.

When possible, you can avoid fishing for clear-water bass by simply finding murky water from inflowing streams or from waves washing against a shoreline. The darker-colored water allows bass to escape bright sunlight and feed aggressively. Look for fish along the mud line where the murky and clear water meet.

Murky Water

The fisherman who finds a patch of murky water in a clear lake may salvage an otherwise wasted trip. But more often, murky water means trouble.

Murky water results from muddy runoff, heavy blooms of algae or plankton, rough fish that root up the bottom or the roiling action of large waves. Many shallow, fertile bodies of water remain turbid year-round.

Murky water confines bass to the shallows. In many murky lakes and reservoirs, weed growth ends at about 6 feet and the water below 12 feet lacks oxygen. But turbidity filters out enough sunlight so bass are comfortable at depths of 4 to 8 feet.

Fishing surveys show that anglers catch bass at a significantly slower rate in extremely turbid water. To check water clarity, tie a white lure to your line, lower it into the water and note the depth at which it disappears. If you can see the lure at a depth of 1 foot or more, chances are you can catch bass.

Stay in the shallows when fishing in murky water. Little sunlight penetrates the cloudy water, so bass remain shallow all day. Target areas with fallen trees, weeds and brush. Keep in mind, however, that bass range farther from cover than they would in clear water. Cast large, noisy lures or those with a lot of flash. Many fishermen carry fine steel wool to polish their spinner blades, and add glitter or reflective tape to their lures.

You should also check out clear streams flowing into murky lakes or reservoirs. These spots provide ideal conditions for bass, especially in summer. The fish find abundant food and cooler temperatures along the edge of murky and clear water.

Fluctuating Water Levels

When avid river fishermen meet to begin a day of fishing, the first question is, "What's the water doing?" They know that even a slight rise or fall can have a big impact on bass location.

Heavy rainfall or a lack of rain causes most water level fluctuations, but there may be other reasons. Irrigation pipes draw huge quantities of water from many rivers and reservoirs during summer. Flood-control reservoirs are drawn down in fall to make room for heavy spring runoff. The Corps of Engineers uses dams to control river levels for purposes of navigation.

A rise in water level causes any fish, including bass, to move shallower; a drop pushes them deeper. Fluctuations affect largemouths in shallow water more than bass in deep water. And a rapid rise or fall has a greater impact on fish movement than a gradual change.

Water levels change quickly in a river following a heavy rain. Bass respond immediately by moving into flooded vegetation near shore. Willows, for example, often become flooded when the water rises. The best way to catch bass in willows is to flip a jig-and-eel or plastic worm as close to the bank as possible and retrieve it through the branches. Flooded brush will hold bass as long as the water is rising or stable. Move your boat slowly just out from the edge and cast a spinner-bait into openings. Or cast parallel to the edge of the brush.

A slight drop in water levels will send bass scurrying to deep water, an instinctive response to avoid being trapped in an isolated pool. To be a successful angler you'll have to move with the fish.

It takes longer for the water level to change in lakes and reservoirs. A slow rise in water level will draw bass toward shore, although it may take several days. The fish remain shallow as long as the water is rising or stable, but they begin to filter into deeper water when the level starts to fall.

Changes in water level can be good or bad for fishing, depending on circumstances. A rise may draw inactive fish out of deeper water. They feed heavily because the flooded shallows offer a new food supply. But in some cases, rising water draws bass into shallow areas, where fishing is impossible.

Bass do not bite as well when falling water drives them deep. But falling water levels may concentrate fish in deep holes or other areas where they are easier to find. For example, if bass are scattered over a shallow flat near a creek channel, falling water would force all of the fish into the channel.

For up-to-date information on water levels, check water gauges, phone the Corps of Engineers or check water stage data in a local newspaper. Water gauges can be found on most large rivers and reservoirs. Look for gauges on bridge pilings or around a dam. Some gauges are marked in one-tenth-of-a-foot intervals, so changes can be detected more easily.

If this information is not available, establish your own reference point on a bridge piling, dock post or other object where a change would be easy to detect. Photographs taken at low water also help you record the exact location of structure and cover that is normally under water. Use a large tree or other object as a reference point when the level returns to normal.

The Spawning Period

Fishermen continually debate the ethics of catching bass on their spawning beds. Most states allow fishing during the spawning period. But some anglers believe that catching spawners is detrimental to the long-term welfare of the bass population. Wherever such fishing is legal, many anglers voluntarily return their bass.

Both male and female bass will bite until spawning time arrives. But they refuse to strike lures while in the act of spawning. Afterward, fishermen catch mostly nest-guarding males. However, anglers in the Deep South often catch big females that appear to be guarding the nest along with the males.

Trophy largemouths bite best just before spawning. Look for them in slightly deeper water adjacent to their spring spawning grounds. More large bass are caught during the pre-spawn period than at any other time of the year. Large bass generally spawn before small ones, so fishermen seeking a trophy should start early in the season. If you catch nothing but small males, it probably means the females have finished spawning and dropped back to deeper water.

To locate spawning areas, cruise slowly through the shallows in a sheltered bay or along a shoreline protected from the wind. Wear polarized glasses to eliminate glare. They not only help you locate the nests, but they also make it easy to see the line twitch when a bass picks up your bait or lure.

Once you've located a nest, make a cast past it. Slowly retrieve your lure into the nest. Allow a jigging lure, like a Texas-rigged soft-plastic lizard or tube jig, to sit on the bottom in the nest. If the nest-guarding bass doesn't immediately grab the lure to take it out of the nest, gently shake the lure in place. Often this tempts the bass into picking up the lure. Once you see the jig disappear in the fish's mouth, or you see your line twitch, set the hook.

If you can't see individual beds because of waves or dark-colored water, simply retrieve a spinnerbait or shallow-running crankbait as close as possible to the edge of the weeds or through other cover types that may hold spawning fish. During this period, bass relate closely to cover and usually refuse to chase a lure into open water.

If spawning bass refuse to hit artificial lures, dangle live bait, such as a nightcrawler, golden shiner or waterdog, in front of nesting bass using a bobber rig. The fish are not interested in eating the bait, but they will pick it up and attempt to move it away if it comes too close to their eggs or fry.

PRE-SPAWN TROPHY BASS are willing biters. After a quick photo, anglers must voluntary practice catch-and-release on these fish to ensure quality bass fishing in the future.

Schooling Bass

When largemouths rip into schools of shad in open water, you can often catch your limit in minutes.

Anglers often encounter schooling bass, or *schoolies*, in late summer or fall while crossing open water on reservoirs. The frenzied feeding is most common in reservoirs with large populations of threadfin or gizzard shad.

Huge schools of shad roam the reservoir to feed on plankton. Schoolies, averaging 1 to 2 pounds each, follow the baitfish, periodically herding them to the surface. Feeding bass sometimes boil the surface for several minutes before the shad escape. To locate schooling bass, look for swirls on the surface and shad skipping across the water. Some anglers carry binoculars so they can watch for diving gulls. The birds swoop toward the surface to pick up shad injured by the feeding bass.

Reservoir fishermen frequently carry a spare rod rigged with a shad-like lure such as a vibrating plug, single-blade propbait, or floating minnow plug. When the bass suddenly appear, they can begin casting immediately without taking time to re-rig.

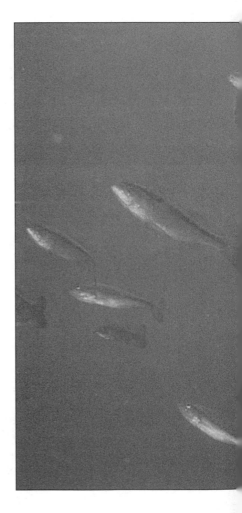

When you spot schooling bass, quickly motor toward the fish, then cut the engine so the boat's momentum carries you toward the school. Use your electric motor to follow the school, staying just within casting range. When the bass sound, try vertical jigging or retrieve a deep-running crankbait through the area where the bass were surfacing.

When you start catching bass from a school, toss them into a live well; throwing them back may spook the school. You can easily keep schooling largemouths alive for the few minutes the frenzy is likely to last, and then throw them back.

Stream Fishing

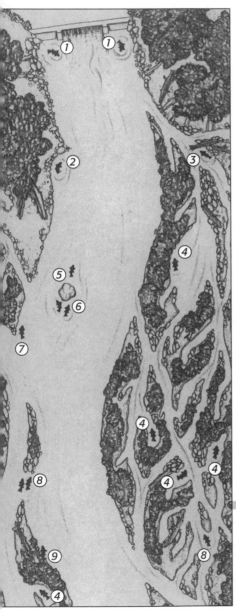

Stream fishermen contend that a bass living in current is a completely different animal than a bass in still water. It looks different, eats different foods and fights better for its size.

Largemouths in streams have sleeker bodies than bass in lakes. They seldom grow as large because they must expend energy just to fight the current. Crayfish, minnows, adult insects and insect larvae comprise a large part of their diet in most streams.

Fishing success on streams is more consistent than on most waters. Cold fronts have less effect on streams and bass continue to bite through summer. Flowing water does not become as warm as standing water and low oxygen levels are rarely a problem.

Fishermen who know how to read the water can easily spot likely holding areas. Bass

BASS LOCATIONS include: (1) eddy below a dam, (2) eddy below a point, (3) below log in a cut, (4) slack-water bays, (5) above a boulder, (6) eddy below a boulder, (7) along edge of water from a tributary, (8) below an island, (9) under an overhanging bank.

162

rarely hold in fast current. They prefer slack water below some type of obstruction. Prime bass locations include eddies, logjams, deep pools and undercut banks. They sometimes feed in a shallow riffle, but usually find a rock to break the current.

Experienced stream fishermen know of certain locations that routinely produce bass. A good example is a fallen tree in a deep pool. If a largemouth is removed, another fish about the same size will soon move in to take its place. Once you discover one of these spots, you will rarely fail to catch bass.

Wading is the best method of fishing a small stream, because it enables you to cover specific areas thoroughly. Most anglers use light spinning gear for casting small jigs, spinners or live bait. The most popular live bait rigs are the simplest: a nightcrawler with a #6 hook on a slip-sinker rig, a minnow with a #4 hook on a split-shot rig, and a crayfish with a #1 hook on a snag-resistant bottom-bouncer rig. Fly-fishing gear works better for drafting insect larvae and other small baits or for dropping lures or baits into hard-to-reach places.

When wading, cast upstream or across the current. Bass seldom strike a lure or bait retrieved against the current, because they are not accustomed to seeing food move in that direction. Work an eddy from the downstream side. Cast into the slack water behind a log or boulder and retrieve the lure or bait along the current margin. Then cover the slack water close to shore. Cast live bait upstream of an undercut bank. Take in line as the current washes the bait toward the overhang. Drift the bait as close to the bank as possible because bass seldom hang in the current. Drift your bait through a riffle by standing downstream of the fast water, then casting above it. Let the current tumble the bait along bottom. Cover the fast water thoroughly, then work the bait through the slack water along both edges of the current.

When fishing in large streams and rivers, use a shallow-draft boat and drift with the current. A trolling motor or outboard can be used to slow your drift, allowing more time to work good spots. Drop an anchor to hold the boat near deep pools that may hold several bass.

Night Fishing

Asked to recall their first night-fishing adventure, most fishermen would tell of tangled lines, snagged lures and bass that got away. No doubt, fishing for large-mouths at night poses some problems. But anglers who fish warm ponds, gin-clear waters or popular urban lakes know that night fishing is often the only way to catch bass. In the latter case, the heavy traffic of water-skiers and boaters drives bass deep during the day, but they move shallow to feed at night.

Bass seldom move far from their daytime haunts to reach nighttime feeding areas. Prime spots include distinct points along shoreline breaks; large, shallow flats extending from shore; and shallow mid-lake reefs. Bass move into the shallows and begin to feed just before dark.

To avoid spooking bass in these shallow areas, place markers during the day. Then sneak in to position your boat in the precise spot after dark.

Night fishing is generally best in summer, especially after a warm, still day with clear skies. On windy, overcast days, bass feed during the day so they may not feed again at night.

Most night fishermen use dark-colored lures that create turbulence or vibration. But some anglers swear by plastic worms. Try surface lures first to catch the active feeders. Bass can easily see the silhouette of topwater lures against

the light background at the surface. Switch to deeper-running lures and work a break leading to deep water after giving surface lures a try. Some fishermen attach a snap to the line, so they can change lures easily without retying.

A slow, steady retrieve works best at night, because bass use their lateral line to home in on the lure. If you use an erratic retrieve, the fish may miss.

Moon phase may have some influence on night-fishing success. Most experts prefer to fish 2 to 3 days on either side of a new moon or a full moon.

6

●●●●●●●●●●●●●●●●●●

PUTTING IT ALL
TOGETHER

Lake Cumberland, KY

A look at the old "braggin' boards" around Lake Cumberland shows that largemouth fishing during the lake's boom cycle in the 50s and 60s was incredible by today's standards. Stringers of 5- to 8-pounders were commonplace, with some as large as 11. You can still catch trophy bass, but the percentage of big ones is much lower.

Largemouths turn on in March, as warming water draws them into the upper ends of creek arms. As a rule, you'll find them farther up the arms than spotted or smallmouth bass.

Most tertiary and some secondary creek arms with shallow, discolored water and brush cover will attract largemouths after a few warm spring days in a row. You'll find them at depths of 5 to 15 feet, often around submerged treetops. On sunny days, they often hold on steep shale banks, where the water is slightly warmer. Don't hesitate to fish under mats of floating debris and pollen, which provide good overhead cover.

Lake Cumberland Physical Data	
Acreage	50,250
Average Depth	80 ft
Maximum Depth	184 ft
Annual Water-level Fluctuation	50 ft
Water Clarity	9 to 20 ft
Limits of Thermocline	30 to 40 ft
Trophic State	oligotrophic

The best way to fish tight pockets in the brush and to penetrate the mats of debris is flippin' with a 3/8-ounce jig-and-pig. Other good pre-spawn patterns are twitching floating minnow plugs on the

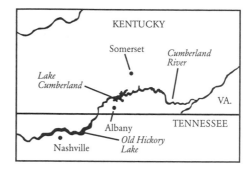

surface, or bulging spinnerbaits along creek arm banks leading into spawning areas.

The fish normally start bedding in mid-April, when the water temperature reaches the mid-60s. They build their nests at depths of 1 to 4 feet, usually on gradually sloping banks with a gravel bottom, and often beneath overhanging tree limbs. Seldom do they spawn where a creek flows in.

If you can see largemouths on the beds, try twitching a floating worm or minnow plug right over them. You may have to skip the worm under limbs to reach the fish.

Bass throughout most of the lake complete spawning by mid-May. As the water warms into the 70s, they move farther down the creek arms, holding at depths of 8 to 20 feet on shoreline points and sharp breaks along the creek channels, especially where you find brush or stumps. Or, they may suspend just off these areas. Work the heavy cover and open water adjacent to it with soft stickbaits or topwaters, using medium-power spinning or baitcasting gear and 10-pound mono.

In early July, largemouths start moving deeper. Look for them on major points in the creek arms or the main lake, generally at depths of 25 to 45 feet. Rounded points with stumps generally hold the most fish. At times, you'll find largemouths suspended off points or bluffs. Summertime fishing can be tough because of heavy boat traffic, especially on weekends, so many anglers prefer night fishing. After dark, the fish move up to depths of 15 to 20 feet on the points. Work these areas with a plastic worm, Texas-rigged with a 1/4- to 3/8-ounce bullet sinker, a jig-and-pig or a 3/8-ounce single-blade spinnerbait. To slow the sink rate and interest bigger bass, try tipping your spinnerbait with a pork chunk.

The summer pattern usually holds until mid-September. Then, largemouths move back up the creek arms and begin feeding more heavily. By early October, you'll find them at the upper ends of major creek arms, especially around downed trees, brush, broken ledge rock, boulders or indentations in the bank. Work water less than 15 feet deep with topwaters, such as buzz baits and chuggers, or try bulging spinnerbaits on the surface. Morning and evening surface action continues until the water temperature drops to 55°F, normally in late November.

When the fish aren't feeding on the surface, try crankbaiting 15- to 25-foot flats adjacent to the creek channels with a deep-diving shad imitation.

As the water continues to cool, bass suspend at depths of 15 to 25 feet over creek channels from 30 to 60 feet deep, or they move into the main lake and suspend off major

OVERHANGING LIMBS provide excellent hiding cover for bass. To reach these fish, skip a plastic worm across the surface of the water and back under the limbs.

points. These suspended fish are tough to catch, but you can take a few by working the edges of the structure with a ¼- to ⅜-ounce jig-and-pig or by jigging a ¼- to ⅜-ounce spoon just off the breakline.

The best time to catch wintertime bass is a day or two after a heavy rain. Warmer, darker water flowing into the head of a creek arm draws bass into 5 to 15 feet of water and turns them on. As long as the water stays warmer than normal, a crankbait or spinnerbait retrieved along the mud line is an effective presentation.

Because the trees were cleared before the lake filled, there's usually no need for heavy tackle. Most anglers prefer spinning gear with 8- to 10-pound mono or a baitcasting outfit with 10- to 14-pound mono, all medium power. For flippin' in heavy brush, however, use a stiff flippin' stick with 25-pound mono.

In Cumberland's clear water, largemouths generally bite best early and late in the day, or whenever the light is low. But from late fall through early spring, the action is fastest on sunny afternoons, when the water is warmest.

Richland-Chambers Reservoir, TX

Trophy largemouth are routine on Richland-Chambers. As one of the country's youngest man-made lakes, the fish population is booming.

In late February, bass begin moving into creek arms off the upper ends of the main creek channels. A few warm days raise the water temperature into the mid-50s and draw the fish onto 5- to 10-foot timbered flats. The lower end of the lake warms more slowly, so bass move into those creek arms 2 to 3 weeks later.

Spawning begins when the water temperature reaches the

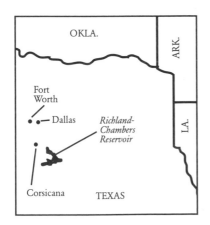

OKLA.

ARK.

Fort
Worth

Dallas

Richland-
Chambers
Reservoir

LA.

Corsicana

TEXAS

Richland-Chambers Physical Data	
Acreage	44,752
Average Depth	24 ft
Maximum Depth	75 ft
Annual Water-level Fluctuation	2 ft
Water Clarity	1 to 5 ft
Limits of Thermocline	20 to 30 ft
Trophic State	eutrophic

low 60s. Look for spawners in 1 to 5 feet of water on a firm, sandy bottom with brushy cover. By late April, all bass throughout the lake have spawned.

During the pre-spawn and spawning period, cast spinnerbaits into the shallows and use a slow-roll retrieve, pausing to let them helicopter alongside brush piles and logs.

Another good technique is twitching a floating minnow plug through the heavy cover.

Bass stay in the creek arms for 10 days to 2 weeks after spawning, but the females are tough to catch. You can take a few fish by casting a crankbait, vibrating plug or Texas-rigged worm, lizard or crawworm onto timbered flats from 5 to 15 feet deep.

By early June, most of the bass have moved back to the main lake. You'll find them at depths of 12 to 20 feet on timbered flats and humps along the main creek channels, along fencerows and submerged road ditches and around points. They also move into the many flooded stock tanks (man-made ponds for watering cattle). The fish are never far from timber or brush.

The surface temperature reaches the 80s by mid-July, forcing bass to retreat to depths of 15 to 25 feet. But they won't be far from their early summer locations. They stay in these spots until early October.

ROADBEDS offer a hard bottom and deep water in the adjacent ditches. They attract largemouths, and sometimes white bass and crappies, in summer.

Texas-rigged worms, lizards and crawworms continue to produce through the summer and into fall. If the bottom is clean enough, try a Carolina rig instead. The lure will drop more slowly, often triggering inactive fish. Another good summertime technique is fishing the brushy cover on deep stock tanks by vertically jigging with a spoon or tailspin, or casting with a jig-and-pig or Texas-rigged worm.

By mid-October, most bass have moved into secondary creek arms. You'll catch them at depths of 15 feet or less using crankbaits, spinnerbaits and topwaters such as prop-baits, buzz baits and chuggers. By early November, fish begin moving into the main creek arms. They often suspend 15 to 20 feet down on heavily timbered flats adjacent to the main creek channels, but you can draw them up with the topwaters just mentioned, or go down to them with jigs, crankbaits or spinnerbaits retrieved slowly.

When the water temperature drops to the low 50s, usually in late December, bass descend into depths of 25 to 40 feet in the main creek channels. Fishing is slow in winter, but you can catch a few fish by vertically jigging a spoon or tailspin to catch bass suspended 10 to 20 feet deep around flooded trees along the channel edges.

A 6- to 7-foot, medium to medium-heavy baitcasting outfit works well for all the techniques mentioned above. Because of the heavy timber and brush, most anglers use 17- to 20-pound (or heavier) line. Use lighter line, about 14-pound test, only when casting crankbaits and minnow plugs in lighter cover.

Shallow-water bass tend to bite best on overcast days with a light breeze. In this kind of weather, fishing is usually good all day long. On calm, sunny days, you'll catch more fish early and late in the day.

Deepwater bass are most active on sunny, breezy days, except in summer, when cloudy weather is best. You'll normally catch more fish in the afternoon than in the morning.

Lake Istokpoga, FL

Bass anglers flock to Florida with one thing in mind: catching a trophy bass. Even though bass over 10 pounds are getting harder and harder to find, there's still a reasonable chance of connecting–if you know when, where and how to go about it.

The biggest bass are caught from mid-December through late March, when the fish concentrate near their spawning areas. They spawn on hard, sandy bottoms in stands of emergent vegetation, particularly bulrushes. Most beds are in water from 1½ to 3 feet deep, with at least 4 feet of water nearby.

Spawning activity is light in December but rapidly gains momentum, peaking a few days either side of the first full moon in March. As with all largemouths, the male moves in first and builds the nest; the female hangs back from the nesting area until just before spawning time. Then she swims onto the nest, accompa-

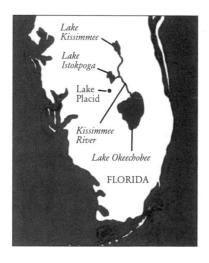

Lake Istokpoga Physical Data	
Acreage	27,692
Average Depth	4 ft
Maximum Depth	10 ft
Water Clarity	2 ft
Color	brownish
Limits of Thermocline	none
Trophic State	eutrophic

nied by one or more males, and deposits her eggs. Females remain on the nest no more than 4 days.

Unlike northern largemouths, the female Florida may assist with nest-guarding duties, especially if the male is caught. Many of the largest Florida bass taken are nest-guarding females.

Because the spawning period is so long and not all bass in the lake spawn at the same time, it's possible to catch some bass in the spawning areas and some in typical summertime habitat on the same day.

Golden shiners probably account for more big Floridas than any other bait. They're most effective in winter, but

they'll catch bass anytime. Wild shiners work better than those raised in hatcheries. Bass prey on wild shiners in nature, so a hooked shiner gets very nervous when a bass approaches. It skitters to the surface and thrashes about wildly, attracting even uninterested bass. A hatchery shiner, on the other hand, has never seen a bass, so it remains much calmer and triggers fewer strikes.

Shiner fishing can be frustrating. Normally, you'll be fishing in heavy cover, either on the edge of a bulrush or cattail bed, over a mat of hydrilla, or in a weed-fringed canal. A lively shiner will tangle your line around the vegetation, and a hooked bass will swim far back into it, so you'll need heavy tackle. A 7- to 9-foot heavy-power fiberglass rod and a good-sized baitcasting reel spooled with 25- to 40-pound abrasion-resistant mono make an ideal combination.

Wild shiners are expensive, but you can catch your own if you know how. To locate shiners, chum shallow weedy areas with oatmeal until you see them dimpling the surface. Then catch them with a cane pole and size 12 hook baited with a tiny doughball, or throw a cast net over them.

Winter fishing usually peaks in midday, when the water temperature is warmest. A slight chop is better than a calm surface; an overcast day better than a sunny one. A warming trend increases feeding activity; a cold front slows feeding and pushes the bass farther back into the rushes or out of the rushes into deeper water.

Fishing for Florida bass on the spawning beds is a highly controversial topic. Many blame this practice for the decline in big bass. When a female bass is on the bed, any disturbance from anglers may cause her to permanently abandon the spawning area. Of course, bass guarding the nest are very aggressive, so many question the sporting ethics of anglers who catch bass when they're most vulnerable.

When the weather warms in summer, wild shiners are tough to keep alive, so almost all anglers use artificials. Most any kind of proven bass lure works—the choice depends on the type of cover, the mood of the bass and personal preference. Serious anglers usually carry several rods rigged with different lures, then experiment to find what the bass want on a given day.

Locating bass in summer can be a challenge in Istokpoga because the lake is so large and has little structure to concentrate the fish. There are thousands of acres of hydrilla-covered flats, any of which may hold bass.

Your best chances of catching bass are early in the morning, when the temperature is coolest. The fish seem to bite better whenever there's a light to moderate wind.

During an intense heat wave, you'll find largemouths in the thickest hydrilla beds and the deepest bulrushes, where the shade keeps the water a few degrees cooler.

The best summertime approach is to cover a lot of water using a "locator" lure, such as a vibrating plug. Once you catch a fish or two, work the area thoroughly with a lure you can retrieve more slowly, such as a plastic worm or a jig-and-pig. On calm days, topwater lures such as prop-baits, buzz baits and minnow plugs twitched along the surface will draw bass out of the weeds. This artificial lure strategy works just as well other times of the year.

When fishing artificials, use medium- to heavy-power bait-casting or spinning gear with 14- to 17-pound mono. Stout tackle helps extract largemouths from the heavy vegetation. When fishing in hydrilla, for instance, it's not unusual to pull in a bass along with a clump of weeds weighing considerably more than the fish.

Starting in October, you'll see bass busting into schools of shad on the surface. A flock of gulls can be a tip-off; they follow close to pick up the injured shad. It pays to carry an extra rod rigged with a topwater lure or a Rat-L-Trap, should this opportunity present itself.

BASS buried deep in hydrilla can be caught by using a plastic worm or jig-and pig.

179

Big Round Lake, WI

The shallow, weed-choked waters of Big Round Lake are heaven for largemouth bass. Better known for numbers than size, the lake has hordes of 11- to 13-inchers. On a good day, you can catch two or three dozen, along with a few 2- to 3-pounders. And there's an outside chance of connecting with a 5- to 7-pounder. Largemouths start to feed heavily in mid-May, about 2 weeks before they spawn. You can find them almost anyplace in the shallows where there are old bulrushes or lily pads, or new growths of coontail or cabbage.

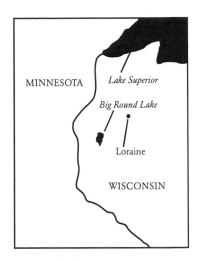

The main draw this time of year is warm water. If you have a temperature gauge, motor along the shoreline and look for warmwater zones. Usually, the bays have the warmest water and draw the most bass. If the water temperature is below 50°F, the fish probably won't be in the shallows.

Another attraction in late spring is spawning sunfish. If you can find a colony of spawning beds, you're likely to find the bass. They move in to feed on crayfish, minnows and other sunfish-egg predators, as well as on the sunfish themselves.

To locate springtime bass, use a shallow-running lure that allows you to cover water quickly, such as a 1/4-ounce tandem spinnerbait. In morning or evening or under other dim-light conditions, try a 1/4- to 3/8-ounce buzz bait or a propbait fished with a reel-and-pause retrieve. When you locate some fish and want to work the area more thoroughly, switch to a 1/4-ounce jig-and-pig.

Big Round Lake Physical Data	
Acreage	1,015
Average Depth	10 ft
Maximum Depth	17 ft
Clarity	1 to 6 ft
Color	green
Thermocline	none

LILY PADS grow on a dark, mucky bottom, and the water around them warms rapidly in spring, attracting pre-spawn largemouths.

In spring, largemouths bite best from midafternoon to dusk, the period of highest water temperature. You'll catch the most fish on warm, still, cloudy days, especially after several days of warm, stable weather. Sunny days with a light breeze can be good too.

By mid-June, the water temperature has risen into the 70s and the weeds are almost fully developed. Under bright conditions, look for bass right in the thickest submerged weedbeds or in the shadiest areas under docks. In low-light conditions, you'll find bass in openings in the weeds, on points along the outside weedlines and around the docks. A few bass remain in the deeper bulrushes.

Use a buzz bait to "call up" bass in the thick weeds; or work a jig-and-pig or Texas-rigged plastic worm through the weeds and along the weedline. Fish the docks with a fat-bodied plastic worm.

When the water greens up during an algae bloom, many of the bass in deep water move shallower. The blanket of algae is so thick it provides shade.

Summertime bass bite best in the same type of weather as in spring. Morning and evening fishing is most productive, especially when you're working the dense weeds; the bass move out of the thick mats and feed along the edges.

By late September, most of the shallow submerged weeds have died. Many bass move into deep clumps of green coontail, although you'll find some in the deeper bulrush beds, particularly those nearest the edge of the break.

Work the edges of a bulrush patch with a 1/4- to 3/8-ounce jig-and pig, occasionally casting back into the rushes to catch less active bass. Use a jig-and-pig, a 1/2-ounce single-spin spinnerbait or a medium diving crankbait to fish the deeper coontail clumps.

Through most of the fall, fishing is best in cloudy weather, just as in spring and summer. But starting in early October, largemouths bite better on sunny, Indian summer days, often right in midafternoon.

Because of the dense weeds in Big Round, most anglers use medium-heavy baitcasting outfits, 6 to 7 1/2 feet long, with 12- to 20-pound mono, depending on the cover. For worm fishing, carry a 6-foot, medium-heavy spinning outfit with 10-pound mono.

Anyone can catch small bass on Big Round, but the big ones are hard to come by. Small bass race after any lure that comes by. The big bass are lazy; they hold tighter to cover and aren't anxious to go out of their way to get food. If they ignore a fast-moving buzz bait, for instance, try slowly retrieving a jig-and-pig in or alongside the weeds.

Upper Mississippi River, MN & WI

The Mississippi's weedy, stump-strewn backwaters are made-to-order for largemouth bass. The fish start to bite in late April, when the water warms to about 55° F. In early season, the warmest water generally holds the most bass.

From late April through May, you'll find bass in beds of green weeds around stumps close to deep water. Work the weeds using spinnerbaits, or run a bright-colored crankbait over the

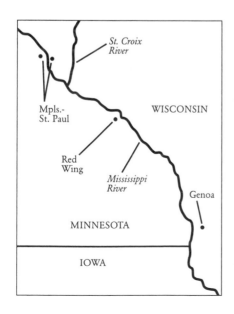

weedtops. For fishing pockets in thick beds of coontail or lily pads, try flippin' with a jig-and-pig. A slower-than-normal retrieve works best in spring.

Weedy backwaters produce bass throughout the summer, but some of the fish move into the main channel and side channels, where there is more current. When changes in weather, such as cold fronts, cause fishing in the backwaters

to slow, bass in these channels continue to bite. The fish are not actually in the current but hold in eddies near current.

Prime channel areas include deep eddies near the head of an island, and wing dams with slow-moving water. You'll also find bass on sand flats near deep water, around beaver houses, along riprapped shorelines or islands and in eddies created by bridge pilings. Few weeds grow in these areas, so most of the bass hang near timber.

Work the timber by flippin' a jig-and-pig or casting a crankbait into an opening, then bumping the wood as you retrieve. Plastic worms and spinnerbaits also account for a lot of bass. When fishing early or late in the day or during a light rain, try retrieving a buzz bait tight to the cover.

In July and August, largemouths may follow schools of surface-feeding shad. You can find the shad by looking for ripples on the surface on a calm day. Select a light-colored lure that you can cast a long way, such as a Sonar, jig or crankbait. Then retrieve it through or just below the shad. Be sure to stay far enough away to avoid spooking the bass.

Bass start to school in September and October. In early fall, you can still catch them in the main channel and side channels, but by mid-September most are moving into the backwaters. Weeds in the backwaters are beginning to die, so bass move into deep holes to find cover and spend the winter. But if you can find green weeds, you'll probably find bass. Another good fall location is a riprapped railroad embankment in the backwaters.

When bass are in deep holes or along deep banks, try a crankbait or jig-and-pig. On a warm, sunny day, they may move up on shallow flats next to the deep water, where you can catch them on spinnerbaits. Use larger baits in fall and work them more slowly than in summer. Fishing stays good until the water cools below 50°F.

During the first few weeks after freeze-up, ice fishermen catch some largemouths in shallow, weedy backwaters. Most bass are taken by accident by pike anglers using tip-ups baited with big minnows, or panfish anglers jigging teardrops tipped with waxworms.

Largemouths bite best during periods of stable weather, although the action is usually fast just before a front. As a

PITCHIN' WEEDLESS JIGS into timber is very effective on Mississippi River largemouths. Point the rod tip down so you can cast with an upward motion; hold the lure in your other hand. Pitch the lure with a low trajectory. To minimize splash, thumb the reel just before the lure hits.

rule, cloudy days are better than sunny ones; mornings and evenings better than midday.

Upper Mississippi largemouths run from 1 to 3 pounds and occasionally reach weights up to 6. They spend a good deal of their time around dense cover, so most anglers use beefy tackle. A medium-heavy 5½- to 6-foot baitcasting outfit with 17-pound mono is a good all-around choice. For pitchin', use a reel with a thumb bar and set the spool tension as loose as possible.

Topwater Lures, 75-77
  Fishing techniques, 127, 148
  When to use, 88, 90, 151, 164, 170,
    175, 179
Touch, Sense of in Largemouth, 11
Trailer Hook, 71
Trees, see: Timber & Brush
Trilene Knot, 65
Trolling,
  Lures for, 79, 80
  Speed trolling, 106
  When to troll, 87, 106, 130
Trolling Motor, 54
Trophy Largemouth, 158, 176
  Baits for, 84, 85
Tuning Lures, 71, 74, 77
  Mis-tuning crankbait, 118
Turnover, 26

U
Undercut Banks, 39, 163

V
Vertical Jigging, 78, 79, 87
  Technique, 107, 119, 141, 148
  When to vertical jig, 107, 118, 141,
    151, 161, 175
Vibrating Blades, 78, 79, 107, 119, 148
Vibrating Plugs, 72, 73, 174, 179, 186
Videos (depth finders), 58
Vision, Sense of in Largemouth, 10

W
Wading, 163
Warm Fronts, 48
Warmwater Discharges, 33, 36
Warm Water, 151
  Fishing techniques, 71, 74, 106
  Lures & baits for, 66, 84, 90, 101,
    106
Warm Weather, 150, 151
  Fishing techniques, 83, 151
  Largemouth locations, 29, 32, 48,
    151, 179
Waterdogs, 85, 86, 159
  Fishing techniques, 119
Water Temperature,
  And largemouth feeding, 12, 170
  And lure selection, 90
  And seasonal bass locations, 24-26,
    29, 31-33, 181
  And spawning, 15, 24

Largemouth preferences, 17
Water Fertility, 17, 18
Weather & Bass Locations, 46-49
Weedguards, 79, 82, 86, 126
Weedless Spoons, 82
  Fishing techniques, 127
  When to use, 90, 138
Weeds & Weedbeds,
  And spawning, 14, 15, 18, 29
  Appearance on depth finder, 59, 132
  Fishing techniques, 71, 87, 101, 124-
    132, 151, 159, 183-185
  In estuaries, 41
  In man-made & natural lakes, 29,
    31-35, 151
  In ponds, 43
  In rivers & backwaters, 37
  Line & equipment for, 87, 126, 179
  Lures & rigs for, 66, 67, 70, 76, 77,
    79, 80, 87, 90, 182
  Types, 121-124
  See also: Emergent & Floating-
    Leaved Weeds
Windy Weather, 48, 151
Winter, 26, 141, 171
  Man-made & natural lakes, 33-35,
    175, 177, 178
  Ponds, 43
  Rivers & backwaters, 36, 186
  Streams, 39
Winter-Kill, 18, 21, 43
Wobblers, 77
World-Record Largemouth, 8
Worms, 84

Y
Yo-Yo Technique, 132

Creative Publishing international, Inc.
offers a variety of how-to books.
For information write:
  Creative Publishing international, Inc.
  Subscriber Books
  5900 Green Oak Drive
  Minnetonka, MN 55343